Life, it's been a Gas

By

Craig Ford

Best Wishes
Craig

ISBN: 978-1-326-71309-6

PublishNation
www.publishnation.co.uk

Dad

A great man, who I miss every hour of every day

I hope this makes you proud x

Acknowledgements

There are a lot of people who helped and supported me in the writing of this book. It was a project I had wanted to do for a long time, and one evening as I sat watching the cricket on the television at home I suddenly grabbed the laptop and started to write. The memories came flooding back, and after getting the help of some statistics in the form of dates and results I never really looked back.

I hope the book helps bring back similar memories of your own time following your favourite football team. Whether it's Bristol Rovers, like mine, or some other team, I'm sure there will be something in here that you can relate to.

I'd firstly like to thank both Kevin and Allan Church, who I discussed the book with on numerous occasions, and who helped jog my memory from time to time – or, more often than not, just confirmed incidents that I had spoken about and planned writing about.

Thanks to my brother Glen, who basically kick-started my allegiance to the Gas. The Gas (or Gasheads) is the nickname given to Bristol Rovers Football Club and their supporters. I suppose it's his entire fault, in a way.

Seriously, I wouldn't have had it any other way. Following a football team has its ups and downs, but it gets you out and about to some far-flung places around the country. I don't think I'd swap the laughs and the close scrapes it's given me for anything, to be honest.

Thanks go to everyone I've encountered along the way. Without them the journey would never have happened … and by everyone I mean everyone I've ever travelled with over the years – either in cars, coaches, minibuses, or on the train. You've all added to the experience.

Thanks to the guys I have spoken to who have helped with advice and ideas. You are all too numerous to mention individually, but if we have spoken along the way over a coffee, a beer, or by email, then this goes out to you.

Thanks to everyone who made my dream come true including the patient guys at Publishnation. It's been hard work at times, but I've really enjoyed it.

Finally, a huge thanks goes to my mother, who helped proofread numerous times and continually encouraged and supported me throughout the project. You're a massive influence on everything I do, and I'm truly thankful.

To all of you: cheers for picking up and looking at my book, whether it's on loan from a library, has been borrowed from a friend, or has been purchased online. You have made my day just by looking at it.

I thank you all.

Introduction

My name is Craig Ford. I am the youngest in a family of five who lived on the outskirts of Hartcliffe in south Bristol. I have a sister Debra and a brother Glen, who are a little over eight and nine years older than me.

Mum was and still is hard-working and immensely house-proud, while Dad worked hard to support his family doing a variety of jobs before eventually working as a successful self-employed plumbing and heating engineer.

As I lived and grew up south of the River Avon in Bristol it would have been natural to expect a young football fan to join the ranks of the Bristol City supporters. After all, City had just been promoted to the old First Division – the Premiership, as it is known today – and most of the other schoolkids had already sworn their allegiance to the red half.

This is the story of falling in love with the game of football – from the early days in the school playground to the first match I attended at Ashton Gate, the home of Bristol City with my father – before ultimately becoming a regular at Eastville Stadium watching my real love, Bristol Rovers Football Club.

I tell the adventure of the early days when I travelled away to watch Bristol Rovers. I tell of the laughs, the tears, and the good times I've encountered as Rovers won promotion and reached their first Wembley appearance in the football club's long history.

I tell of the disappointments of relegation, of dropping out of the Football League in 2014, and of the joy of bouncing back after a promotion-winning day at Wembley Stadium just twelve months later.

And I tell the stories of close encounters with rival supporters, of the music and the fashion of the day, and what it was like to feel part of a football club you had grown to call your own.

Following Bristol Rovers on the road also became a great asset at school. Geography became one of my strongest school subjects as I travelled up and down the motorway whizzing past far-flung places on the map of Great Britain, while in the early days listening to big European games on the radio helped my awareness of European cities.

The book covers the ups and downs of life as a Bristol Rovers supporter in a way every football fan can relate to every Saturday afternoon throughout the length and breadth of the country, whatever their team. Going to an away game was an adventure. You never knew what to expect, what you were going to see, or what you might encounter. It was an exciting prospect, and I couldn't wait for the next one to come.

Sit back, put the kettle on, and read what it was like for me to follow the club I loved, as we bounce around the Football League stadiums of England.

Chapter One

Blue Blood, Red Blood

It was the start of what was to become the long, hot summer of 1976. Unbeknown to me at that particular time Bristol City had just won promotion to the old First Division. It was the holy grail – top-flight football – and it was all happening less than two miles from my own backyard.

It meant nothing to me at the time. I had yet to get interested in football, and I couldn't tell you what division any team was in at that time – and, to be honest, I couldn't even name a famous footballer, as I was still in the cocoon of childhood.

My brother was a football fan – a Bristol Rovers supporter – and had started his allegiance to the blue half of the city when he was taken to Eastville Stadium, the home of Rovers, to watch a match as a youngster by our Uncle Mervyn.

Now let me introduce you to a few people who laid the foundations of the story I'm about to share with you.

Our Uncle Mervyn was a blue, a true Rovers supporter, and he is our uncle from my mum's side of the family. He was a keen Bristol Rovers fan back then, as he still is today, and was a regular at many of the Rovers home games until recently.

My mum grew up in central Bristol – the St Pauls district, in fact – so Eastville Stadium, the home of Bristol Rovers as it was back then, would have been no more than a stone's throw away. Mervyn was her older brother, and he had always – as long as she can remember – shown an interest in football, particularly that of Bristol Rovers. So the blue bloodline that I was eventually to have can initially be traced back from this route.

When my mum and dad were married back in August 1957 they

3

lived together in a flat along the Stapleton Road in Eastville, Bristol. Mum's brother Mervyn had also married, and lived in the district of St Anne's at the time. Mervyn used to ride over and drop his bicycle off at their home in Stapleton Road before walking the short distance up the street to watch the football.

Mum and Dad often told me stories as I grew up of watching the massive hordes of football supporters as they headed off towards the Rovers ground for the match. Attendances at Rovers home matches were at an all-time high during this period. Numbers attending matches were often in the mid 20,000 mark, and cup ties could see well over 30,000 supporters in attendance. A fine example was the time the famous Matt Busby's Busby Babes of Manchester United came to visit Bristol back at the start of 1956. A crowd of 35,872 watched Bristol Rovers destroy Manchester United 4–0 at Eastville Stadium in a third round FA Cup tie. It was to be one of the more successful periods in the history of Bristol Rovers, as they challenged for promotion from the old Second Division with hope of joining the elite in the First Division.

It was the start of the Bert Tann era. Bert Tann was the Rovers manager from 1950 to 1968, a spell of eighteen years, and he still remains the longest-serving post-war manager at Rovers to date.

Bristol is a large city. As in many large cities across Britain and on the Continent there are a lot of split loyalties among families, and ours was one that had them. Mum came from the north side of Bristol, which is traditionally the side of town that supports Bristol Rovers, while Dad grew up south of the river in Bedminster Down, and he would have been more inclined to back the red half (namely Bristol City). Neither were football mad but they had their family influences, which swayed them towards either supporting Rovers or City …

Although, having said that, my dad would never pin his colours on any one team. He stayed pretty impartial, and he was happy enough to see both teams doing well. Dad was happier watching the more mellow sport of cricket, which is why I was also to become a fan of this sport in later years. From the late 1990s we attended many matches together, watching Gloucestershire County Cricket Club at Nevil Road in Bristol, and were also lucky enough to see a few

England internationals at the same venue.

Uncle Mervyn took my brother Glen along to the Bristol Rovers home matches for a while, but it wasn't too long before Glen was old enough and confident enough to attend Bristol Rovers home matches on his own and Glen would take the long bus ride across Bristol to visit Eastville Stadium..

He was lucky enough to have witnessed the Watney Cup triumph over Sheffield United, and the successful promotion season of 1973/74 as his early introduction to the Gas (as we are fondly named).

The name Gas, or Gasheads, as the club and its supporters are known, came about because the home of Bristol Rovers at Eastville Stadium was located in close proximity to the gasworks. It was often said that the smell of gas would occasionally drift across the pitch during a game.

History states that rivals Bristol City gave Rovers the name Gas as a derogatory term, but it was soon adopted with great affection, and all Rovers supporters proudly call themselves Gasheads today.

I can just about remember Glen keeping a scrapbook of all the local *Bristol Evening Post* reports, along with seeing the odd football programme lying around our shared bedroom. I can't recall much else of that time, as I would have been still spending most of my time reading *Beano* comics, or watching Spider-Man and other kids' cartoons on the television.

My brother is almost nine years older than me, so I was yet to fully understand that he was actually a Bristol Rovers supporter, or where he disappeared at the weekend. Being his younger brother, and being only around five years old at the start of the 1973/74 season, I can fully understand why at that time he tried to hide away his entire Bristol Rovers programme collection. I was often caught out scribbling over them, so it was a wise move to keep as many of them out of my reach and harms way.

Back to 1976, and the promotion of rivals Bristol City. They had arranged the customary open-top bus tour of a promoted team, and were expected to tour around the streets of south Bristol. I can't recall when or where the open-top bus tour actually went, but it was to pass by our humble abode and I was to be the unknowing bait.

Now when I say 'bait' I don't mean 'bait as in some kind of Rovers v. City mass brawl', but I was being used as a pawn in a plan of my brother. The plan must have been to show that there were still plenty of Rovers fans about.

'Come 'ere, Craig,' would have been the call to me, I'm sure. 'Put this scarf on your bike and go out and ride along the main road to see if you can see the City's open-top bus.'

'Yeah, OK.'

Little did I know: I was a small kid who had just started at junior school. I didn't understand or know what was happening. Now I can remember the scarf my brother proudly tied to the handlebar of my Tomahawk bike. It was a silk scarf proclaiming the famous Bristol Rovers strike duo of Warboys and Bannister.

Off I went pedalling along the main road, without a care in the world, in search of an open-top bus. I didn't get far: the scarf managed to catch in my bicycle chain and brought me to a sudden halt. I wobbled, and almost fell from the bike. The scarf had wedged itself between the sprocket and the chain, and I wasn't going anywhere. I remember gingerly dragging the bike back home with the scarf still mangled up in the chain, wondering if I was to be greeted by an angry brother.

Well, to be honest, I can't remember what happened. I'm sure he kept it reasonably quiet from Mum and Dad as it wasn't a good idea, really, was it? Sending his small brother off into the lion's den like a lamb to the slaughter wouldn't have gone down too well.

The scarf was ruined. I remember it was full of holes and covered in oil. I never did get to see that bus, so never knew what lay in store for me on that particular evening. If any rival fans had seen this happening I'm sure they would have found it most amusing and, to be honest, I think it probably could have been reminiscent of a scene from *Candid Camera*, the popular television show of the time.

There was another time around the same period when my good old brother pinned a team photograph of the current Bristol Rovers team on to a large, square piece of chipboard, and presented it to me rather proudly. A very nice job it was too. However, that was no ordinary

6

piece of chipboard. It was my ramp, which I used to catapult myself up into the air Evel Knievel-style.

Evel Knievel was a famous stunt bike rider of the time, and I was more likely to see him as an early idol than any local footballer in those days. So the picture had to go – much to the disappointment of my brother, I'm sure. He had yet to get me on board as a young Rovers fan. I wasn't coming easy, that's for sure.

Now as an eight-year-old boy who had yet to pin his colours on the wall, and who had yet to fall into the lifelong trap of supporting a football team, there were still times when one would have thought I could have been heading down the red path.

I remember unwrapping a red and white scarf at Christmas one year. Who bought me it? I haven't a clue, to be honest. There is a lot of red in the family from Dad's side, so the scarf must have come from one of my dad's brothers. Maybe it was Uncle Jeff or Uncle Cliff, who were both City fans, or more likely one of his sisters my Auntie Betty or Auntie Lorraine. Our Auntie Lorraine was also a keen City supporter, and was in fact a season ticket holder at Ashton Gate for many years.

I can't honestly ever recall putting it around my neck. Maybe, if I had, my brother would have done something about it … probably hanged me with it. Who knows?

As we entered the 1976/77 season something was about to change. It was to be the year that I finally was going to be shown the delights of professional football.

Dad was never a massive footy fan when we were kids and, to be honest, apart from the games we persuaded him to attend over the years (and that wasn't very many) I don't think he would have bothered too much with football. The only time he set foot near a football pitch was to watch Bristol Rovers at Christmastime, or when Bristol Rovers made it to Wembley for the first time.

In later years he enjoyed watching his grandson Wayne (Glen's son) play football on Sundays in the local youth league. It wasn't that Dad wasn't interested in football. It was just that he had other interests, and didn't have much time for it at that time of his life.

So, as I said earlier, it was now the 1976/77 season. We had Bristol City in the old First Division, and Bristol Rovers were playing in the second tier of English football.

At Whitehouse junior school I was now becoming a regular playground footballer. We would spend all our morning breaks and lunch hours kicking a tennis ball around. I'm sure back then we were all reasonably good players, as trying to stop, control, pass, and shoot a small tennis ball was no easy feat. As I grew more confident I became a regular little goalscorer on the school playground, and was now becoming one of the first kids picked by the playground captains.

The captains were usually the kids who had taken the trouble to bring the ball to school, so understandably they were always going to have a big say in who was in the teams. I enjoyed my new popularity, and looked forward to our regular football runaround.

We had a fair-sized playground, and it was almost fully enclosed by a small red-bricked wall. It wasn't a high wall but big enough to chalk on the width of a goalmouth, and it also stopped the ball disappearing to all corners of the playground.

I remember we played either at the top end of the playground or at the bottom. If we were quick enough out of the classroom at the sound of the bell we could nab the top end of the playground. This was the best place to play, as it was enclosed on three sides by a wall, and had been marked out for the game Bulldog. We could utilise these markings as the goal area.

The playground staff monitors – or dinner ladies, as we knew them – favoured the girls having this area. So we were not always lucky enough to grab it first, and usually had to settle for the bottom end of the playground.

The bottom end of the playground was only enclosed by a wall on two sides, and had a large gap at one corner that led out towards the staff car park. Everyone had to be careful not to lose the ball here, as it was an area that was out of bounds. We did, however, have the use of the end of the school building as one of our goalmouths and, if my memory serves me correctly, I am sure the wall was the end of the headmaster's office. He must have regularly heard the thump of the ball hitting his wall.

Oh, well, he never did come out. I expect he was just pleased we were all getting along and playing nicely.

I was beginning to get the football bug. I remember coming home from school and running down the local shops to purchase the football collector cards. There were a couple of strips of pink bubblegum inside the packets as well, but I just wanted to see which players I had. The cards were made up of all the players from the teams in the First Division.

The big two in those days were Liverpool and Manchester United. Liverpool were almost unbeatable back then. They were starting their period of domination of English and European football.

The kids in school were either Liverpool or Manchester United fans. There were also a fair few City fans around as well, but I took no interest in them. I never pinned my colours with any team: I still hadn't, at that time, chosen anyone.

Back then we didn't have football on the television 24/7. The only games we saw were *Match of the Day* and Sunday's *The Big Match*. *Match of the Day* was still a little late for me on Saturday evenings, so I mainly watched Sunday's afternoon's edition of *The Big Match* on ITV.

The Big Match was normally focused on the London sides, if I remember rightly. It seemed that West Ham, Chelsea, and Spurs were the only sides ever on.

After watching the football on the TV I would set up my on football pitch on the living room carpet. I would make two goal nets with pencils, and then pick two sides to play against each other using my football collector cards. The two sides would line up, and the game would begin. The ball was a marble, and I would pass the marble around between the cards and thoroughly enjoy myself playing my imaginary game – my very own *Match of the Day*, or *The Big Match*.

I got quite into this, and made up leagues and played out matches. I wrote the scores down and updated the league tables as we went from game to game. I began to write team names down and cut them up, and make pretend cup draws. I'm sure this was a massive help at the time to my schooling. Spelling, writing … it must have helped. The teachers would have loved it, I'm sure.

I can just about recall my junior school having a school football team and occasionally playing football, but I can't recall ever knowing that a game had been arranged. I can remember once walking home from school and seeing the pitch being readied for a school match. Why didn't I get to hear about this?

It seems strange, but I can remember that the game was between my junior school, Whitehouse Junior School, and the local school about half a mile down the road, which was Red House. It's strange I should remember that, but it must only be because of the names of the schools. They were not hard to remember … the two colours: one white and one red….

I wandered over to watch for a while. Our school pitch was on a slope so, as you can imagine, the ball was always down one end. And, in typical schoolboy football fashion, everyone was just chasing after the ball. Maybe this is why I didn't play: no organisation. Mr PE teacher would have needed to sort it out before I was going to grace it with my skills. It seemed strange that it was played on the school's sloping pitch, as there was a perfectly flat top pitch higher up the school field. That flat pitch happened to be the very pitch that we all played on after school and at the weekends, having our kickabout with my mates.

Sometimes it would be small groups of us playing 'Wembley', as we called it, or a mass 20 v. 20 'Anything goes' game, with kids of all ages from around the estate.

These games could get a little tasty at times, so you had to have your wits about you and not try and tackle or beat the bigger kids too often, as it usually led to a sly kick or a fairly hard shove next time you had the football at your feet. We had some great matches that went on for hours, until it was impossible to see any more as darkness fell.

Anyway, as I watched the school game for a while longer I decided to head off back home. There was nothing to see, and it wasn't actually *The Big Match*, was it?

Chapter Two

My First Game

Football was now becoming a much bigger part of my life, and I had started to know the names of the players from the big First Division sides. I had also started to take notice of Liverpool Football Club. When I say 'take notice', I wasn't becoming a supporter of them. I was just seeing them as the big, successful side they were.

My playground footballing career was still blooming, and I had started to practise my skills in the driveway and garden of our house. We were lucky that the gates could act as a goalmouth at one end, while the garage door was the other. Unfortunately this wasn't really an idea football pitch, as many matches were interrupted at a fairly early stage due to the crash of the ball thundering into the metal garage door.

'Get over the school,' was the cry that often came from either Mum or Dad. The gates weren't much better, either, as a wayward shot sailed over the low gates and into the street or a neighbour's garden.

When I look back now, I must have been the most annoying of the kids in the street. Most of the neighbours' kids had grown up. Some had even flown the nest, and I was the youngest left in our small cul-de sac. They must have been on pins watching the ball fly around the gardens just missing their cars, their prized flower beds, and their large front room windows. The back garden of our house also became my football pitch, with the washing line posts acting as the goalposts. Again the call regularly came up,

'Get over the school with that ball. This isn't a football pitch.' But it was a football pitch. It was my football pitch, and it was to be my home football pitch for a number of years. I had started my own imaginary football team now, and had made up a fixture list with teams from the old Division Four.

I was the main striker, and I had picked and signed players from other clubs and played out the fixtures in the garden. It didn't do the grass much good, as Dad often came home from work and told me off about the worn, muddy areas of his lawn.

Over the years I would reach the dizzy heights of the First Division, winning FA cups and League One titles. I had great fun doing that over a number of years. I probably kept that book running right up until I reached my teens. We went by the imaginary name of Bristol West.

So the grass regularly became a little muddy, and an odd shed window or pane of glass was broken in the greenhouse as the imaginary seasons progressed, but I can look back on it as a fond childhood memory. It would not have been so fond a memory or very much amusement for Dad at the time, that's for sure. The number of times the football bounced over or was accidentally kicked over the neighbours' gardens wouldn't have gone down too well, either.

I would leap the garden fences to recover the ball from a number of nearby gardens without a second thought. I'm sure they would have been pulling their hair out as a young Craig darted around their back gardens collecting his lost ball.

I was now beginning to go to bed early so that I could listen to the midweek football commentary on the radio. The big European nights were something else, and I still look back on listening to those nights with a tingle.

Football on the radio back then was brilliant. It was the best way to get a football fix. As I said before, there was no football on every television channel you could shake a stick at back then.

Radio 2 was the highlight of any football nut, both midweek and at weekends. The local radio stations were still not broadcasting live games from around the grounds like they do today. It was only brief reports or score flashes for us to know how our sides were getting on.

Radio 5 and Radio 5 live still use the same tune before reading the football results out on the radio – 'Out of the Blue' by Hubert Bath – as Radio 2 did back then.

The radio I used to listen to it on was a big beige radio, probably from the 1950's. I can't recall where it came from, but I had a sneaky feeling it came from my gran. I never had it there long, as it was such a big lump on the bedroom dresser. I was to be bought my very own Alba radio cassette player soon after.

If that old radio was still around today I'm sure it would have been worth a bob or two to a collector. I expect it was either given away or smashed up and thrown out in the dustbin.

The end of the season was in sight and I was now staying up later, and sometimes was able to watch the football highlights on *Match of the Day*. Mum would go off to bed, and Dad would sit downstairs with me while we watched the football.

As I said earlier, Liverpool were the team of the time, and we both used to enjoy watching them as they were roared on by the swaying Kop at Anfield. I remember that Ray Clemence was Liverpool's number one at that time, and there were also Emlyn Hughes, Kevin Keegan, and a guy who was Liverpool's supersub: David Fairclough.

Dad used to call Ray Clemence 'Smiler', as he always seemed to have a grin or smile across his face. On looking back, it was probably because he didn't have anything to do most weeks. Liverpool rarely had trouble putting teams away.

Kevin Keegan was emerging as England's new superstar, leading the line at Liverpool and on the international stage for England. Emlyn Hughes was also a bit of a smiley character, if I remember rightly.

The guy I remember the most, strangely enough, is the ginger-haired supersub David Fairclough. The guy always seemed to come on from the bench and score a vital goal that either pulled Liverpool back into a game or won it for them.

I had now started asking Dad to take me to a live football game, and kept on to him at regular intervals. I'm sure he was hoping Glen would take me but he was unlikely to want his little brother hanging around at that stage, and maybe Mum wouldn't want me travelling across town with him at such a young age.

I was still throwing the odd hint that I would like to see a live football match, but neither my brother nor our dad took me. I think that these nights watching football together was slowly working its magic on my dad, though, and soon I was to see the mighty Liverpool at first hand. My first game was only a matter of time away. Now I'm not saying I was a Liverpool fan – far from it – but how many of us can say our first professional live football game was against the English and future European Champions? I can.

My first game was to be Bristol City v. Liverpool at Ashton Gate on 16 May 1977. Now I'm not proud to say that I saw City before Rovers, but I wasn't there for them: I was there to see Liverpool.

The Liverpool side that night included the great names of Ray Clemence, Phil Neal, Alec Lindsay, Tommy Smith, Ray Kennedy, Emlyn Hughes, Ian Callaghan, Jimmy Case, David Fairclough, David Johnson, and Terry McDermott. Now that was some introduction to the live games, wasn't it? Kevin Keegan was not in the team that night. I can only imagine he was either carrying a knock or was being rested for their European Cup Final.

I remember sitting on my dad's shoulders for the majority of the match in a decent-sized crowd of 38,688. I can't recall the match, but as I arrived at the match I remember the excitement I was feeling, knowing at long last I was at a football match – a real, proper football match. The noise, the pushing, and the sheer volume of people stick in my mind. I was hooked now, and things would never be the same again.

My first Bristol Rovers match was just a few months away: it was to be at Eastville Stadium.

Eastville Stadium had a character all of its own. It was a large stadium, mainly because of the wide track running around the outside of the pitch. Both speedway and greyhound racing also shared the stadium with football.

The large Tote End and the Muller Road open end could hold a large number of supporters, and the atmosphere for big games there was unique.

I hadn't changed. I was still asking to go to the football, but Dad wasn't really interested. He was a busy guy working to look after his family, and football wasn't his priority. Eventually I was to get another chance to see a game, and this was to be the start of a lifelong affection for Bristol Rovers.

Saturday 3 December 1977 was to be the day I first watched Bristol

Rovers. It was to finish as a 1–1 draw with Hull City in the Second Division.

I know that Billy Bremner was in the Hull City side that afternoon – not because I can remember him playing, but due to the songs I heard that day. The songs were mainly sung to and about Billy Bremner, and they were not favourable ones towards him either. Billy Bremner would have been at the end of his career back then and, according to record books I've since checked, he retired from playing in the summer of 1978.

The overwhelming memory of this first game was the vast Tote End, with its tall, long sweeping steps that seemed to go back and across for miles. The Tote End was so named due to it being used as a tote betting area for the greyhound race nights. The whole stadium looked huge to me. The two stands on either side of the pitch and a large away end, with the M32 motorway riding past it, gave it a wonderful open feel.

As we stood on the Tote End the players came out to our left, and I remember that the south stand, which ran the length of the pitch to our right, had a strange lump on its roof (that's the best way I can describe it). It was a strange sight indeed, and I later learnt it was the press box.

Another lifelong memory of Eastville that has always stuck with me was the smell of hot dogs and onions being fried and sold on small silver carts. The smoke and steam would float up into the air, giving everyone the aroma of what was being prepared for the mass of hungry football fans. It was a smell that I had never come across before, but it was a smell that even to this day I associate with Eastville Stadium and the matches I attended there.

So my football journey had begun, and it was the start of a fun roller coaster ride.

Chapter Three

First Hero, First Cup Run

The first games had now come and gone, so it was now time to keep up the pressure on both my brother and my dad to regularly take me along to the football at the weekend. I was still fighting a losing battle with Dad, as he was always too busy either working, or running around with Mum as they did their weekly shopping chores. So it was to be my brother Glen who was going to have to face my constant whining.

'Football today …'

'Rovers are home today …'

'Are we going?' This sort of thing was usually answered with:

'We will see later.' Or 'Not sure yet.' This, to be honest, was probably worse than an actual 'Yes' or 'No', as it just kept me in limbo. But I knew that if I kept the pressure up then surely he would eventually cave in, and we would both be off to watch the Rovers.

I can remember that most weekends Mum and Dad would return home from shopping around midday or just after, and would usually return with fish and chips for all of us. It was a great opportunity (as we sat down together to eat our dinner) to work my magic and apply some more pressure.

'Are we off to the football?' I would enquire. I remember Dad would give me 50 p and say to my brother,

'Are you taking him today?' It didn't always result in a positive outcome, but when it did then I was happy.

When I didn't attend the matches I kept up with what was happening at Eastville by listening to the local radio sports news and the Saturday sports programme, which started at 1 p.m. The waiting and anticipation were almost like waiting for Christmas as the morning dragged. All I wanted was for the sport to start, and I was happy. I had also started to read the local *Bristol Evening Post*, reading up on the local football news. I still pick up a paper today, whether it's a national or local publication, and always start on the back pages first, working from right to left. It's a habit that I've never got out of.

Back then Bristol Rovers had a young local teenage striker leading the front line named Paul Randall. Paul Randall was to become my first footballing icon as a young boy, and he was the player I wanted to be on the school playground kickabouts. Bristol Rovers, if only in my eyes, seemed to revolve around him and his goals.

Paul Randall was a natural goalscorer, and his overall contribution to our team's success was massive. He had been signed from a local non-league side, Frome Town, at the start of the 1977/78 season. I have since read his autobiography, and learnt that he once turned down a call to sign for Bristol City in favour of Rovers. Now surely that deserves a lasting statue to a hero.

Back in those early days at Eastville I can remember watching some of the English well-supported big name clubs. Bristol Rovers traded punches in Division Two alongside Newcastle, Southampton, Sunderland, Crystal Palace, West Ham, and Chelsea in my first few seasons as a Gashead. It almost seems impossible now to think that back then we were on the same reasonably level playing field as such teams. I suppose it happened again on a similar (if slightly smaller scale) during our Twerton Park days, but that's a story for later.

Both Newcastle United and Sunderland supporters always brought large followings, and it's the fans of these clubs who taught me the theory behind the physics of light and sound.

As a kid I remember standing amazed at the noise generated from the travelling supporters of both Newcastle and Sunderland. The puzzling thing that I learnt from these encounters was that light travels faster than sound. As the supporters clapped and sang their songs it always seemed that their hands were apart as the noise of the clapping hit the Tote End. Brilliant. I was learning better out of school than in it. The football stadium had become a top-rated classroom, and there was not a teacher in sight. I have always said that my world geography was taught to me by following football clubs and countries from around the world. The European cup ties and the venues were a lesson in themselves.

Never stop a young lad from following his football. It's amazing what can be learnt. It wasn't only science and geography lessons that I was learning. I was also learning that it was a pretty tough life on the terraces back in those days. It was the height of football violence and terrace fashion, and in general not many weekends went past without a scuffle or two breaking out somewhere around the stadium.

Saturday 28 January 1978 was FA Cup day. Bristol Rovers had reached the fourth round of the cup after knocking out Sunderland away at Roker Park. This was a mini cup upset in its own right, and was a decent result, as Rovers were not the best of travellers and Sunderland was a long way away (and in front of their own crowd they were a difficult side to beat). The reward for this result was a tasty-looking tie at home to Southampton. Thankfully I had managed to pressure the powers that be at home, and I was being taken to the game by my brother.

We left in good time and arrived to take up our places in the North Terrace enclosure. I remember taking up my position near or around the halfway line, propped up against the perimeter fencing with all the other young kids of my age. I didn't know anyone but was soon feeling at home, chatting away with the lads – with whoever happened to be standing alongside me that day – about the football, about which player was going to score the winning goals, and general kiddie chit-chat.

One thing I remember about this part of the stadium was that there was a channel which dropped away in front of the perimeter fencing, and you always had to avoid standing in it for a couple of reasons. If I happened to drop into the void space it would probably mean that, as I was only a four-foot-tall kid, I wouldn't be able to see over the fence and watch the game unfolding in front of me. What would have been just as frustrating is that if it had been raining the void space tended to be filled with water, and it was likely that I would have ended up with wet trainers and wet socks to go with them. Never a good combination on a cold winter's afternoon, is it? I had stood in that position many times, so had learnt the hard way.

Bristol Rovers were the underdogs that day, playing against a Southampton side who were on the up, and who had won the FA Cup only two years earlier. The Southampton line-up that day included Alan

Ball, who would end up playing for Bristol Rovers some years later, when he was signed by manager Bobby Gould in January 1983 during his first spell as Bristol Rovers manager. The form book was to be thrown out of the window that afternoon as Rovers ran out comfortable 2–0 winners, with both the goals coming from Paul Randall. It was a game that probably alerted other clubs to the present of the young Rovers striker, and I expect teams kept a close eye on him from that day.

The pending victory of Rovers had touched a raw nerve, and it had sparked up a number of the travelling Southampton supporters to unwisely take the decision to invade the pitch from the Muller Road end of the stadium where they were standing, possibly in the hope of the game being abandoned. It was to be the first real outbreak of football violence I was to encounter.

As the game neared its conclusion a number of Saints fans began climbing the Muller Road fencing and started spilling on to the track that wound its way behind the goal. I can see them now in their fake sheepskin and leather jackets bouncing around and waiting for their numbers to increase. A few ran on to the pitch but didn't really know what to do next, as the stewards in their orange jackets (along with the police) pushed them back in no time at all. The referee had stopped the game temporarily but it couldn't have been for more than a couple of minutes, as the Southampton fans disappeared back into their section. The sight of a large number of Bristol Rovers fans gathering at the Tote End of the stadium and climbing over from their places on the terrace seemed to bring them to their senses pretty quickly.

A few scuffles broke out with the stewards and the police as they walked back along the touchline, along with a fair amount of pushing and shoving while order was soon restored. I remember looking across to the Tote End that day, and I can still see the first Rovers fan, who was wearing a pair of beige trousers, climbing over the fencing ready to chase back the invading Saints. It's funny how certain things just stick in your memory, isn't it? The sheer numbers of Southampton fans that day could have easily overrun the stewards, but they seemed happy enough just to put up a token gesture. It was the start of things to come, as I grew up watching football during the infamous days of football violence at its worst.

The game that day was, in my opinion, the one which promoted Paul Randall into the media limelight both at a local and nation level. I'm sure it was the start of other clubs sniffing around him, and it would sadly (in the opinion of a Rovers supporter) eventually lead him to moving on to Stoke City the following season, where he became a First Division player. The day he left I remember being pretty upset that my favourite player was moving on. Thankfully we still had him for another few months, and as a football supporter you learn to get used to losing players and managers who you like. It happens so many times that you just become hardened to it in the end. As I now see, it's a game and their livelihood, so who in their right mind would turn down the chance of a better work position with higher wages?

Next up in our mini cup run were First Division Ipswich Town, managed by the future England boss Bobby Robson. Ipswich Town were a decent side and had some big name stars that season, including Paul Mariner, Mick Mills, John Wark, Brian Talbot, George Burley, and Clive Woods, to name a few. Unfortunately I didn't make this game. All the keeping on and the charm didn't get me a ticket for the game, so I had to cheer them on by listening to the local radio coverage. It was a snowy weekend, so maybe that had a bearing on why we didn't travel across town to attend the game.

Bristol Rovers had another decent 20,000 plus crowd at Eastville, and were very much up for the challenge. They were to come very close to causing another cup upset that afternoon, as they ran Ipswich Town very close, and if it hadn't been for a questionable referee call that day who knows how far they could have gone in the cup that season.

The Rovers had led deep into injury time before Ipswich Town equalised and grabbed a 2–2 draw, and eventual victory over us in the replay back at Portman Road. The jumping around and shouting at home in my bedroom did no good, as our cup run had ended. And with this loss came disappointment, as we had come so close to knocking out a First Division side. Ipswich Town went on to Wembley that season and lifted the FA Cup by beating Arsenal 1–0 in the final. I suppose we could say we were beaten by the eventual winners. No consolation really, but it was something to grab on to, wasn't it? It should have been us!

Chapter Four

The Early Days As a Gashead

The next few seasons would coincide with a traumatic period in the history of Bristol Rovers Football Club but, to be honest, I think that most periods could be labelled as traumatic. There was the Eastville south stand fire, relegation from the Second Division, and the growing concern over the lease at Eastville with the Bristol Stadium Company (with the real prospect of becoming homeless). This period would also see me travel to my first away games and become much more of a regular at Eastville and on the road, as I became much more independent.

The 1978 season started with a tidy home win (3–1) over Fulham at Eastville. It was one of the rare occasions that I sat out at the Muller Road end of the stadium alongside the away fans. It was the start of the season and the weather was still pretty good, so why not? That summer had also seen the World Cup, which had been held in Argentina, and I remember staying up to watch some of the games. England had failed to qualify but Scotland was there, so we tended to sit around as a family and watch them. I can't say I remember much about the tournament, but the Archie Gemmill goal against Holland springs to mind. Check it out if you haven't seen it for a while. It's a goal that is hard to forget, and is worth watching. Peru's funny red and white shirts and the ticker tape reception the host nation received during their games also spring to mind when thinking about the 1978 World Cup (or was the ticker tape just at the final?).

There are a few more Bristol Rovers games from that 1978/79 season that I can recall, including a hat-trick from Paul Randall in a 4–1 victory against Blackburn Rovers, a 2–0 win over Newcastle United, where I started learning physics (as I've mentioned earlier), and an amazing 5–5 home draw against Charlton Athletic on a chilly afternoon standing in the Tote End. West Ham came that season as well. All I remember from their visits over the next couple of seasons was the fighting on the Tote End terracing as the two rival groups of supporters fought running battles, oblivious of the football match being played out on the pitch in front of us. Luckily I was young enough not to take a whack, so I suppose I felt pretty safe. The Tote End was a vast terraced end, so you could just stand back and watch the events unfold.

It's strange to think that back then football violence was a big cancer running through the national game. It was something I saw regularly, and became almost accustomed to. I can't recall it being something that I was frightened of, or that it was even going to stop me from attending a game. Kids don't see danger, so they say.

There were no other notable games during that season, and Rovers didn't even have an FA Cup run for any of us to get excited about. Strangely enough it was Ipswich Town again who were to knock Rovers out, pretty convincingly, 6–1 at Portman Road. My brother travelled up to this evening game on a train, which I would imagine had been laid on by Bristol Rovers as a football special. It's a shame clubs don't do this any more. I expect it was actually British Rail that pulled the plug on it. They probably lost more money than they made due to damage to their carriages, and of course privatisation would have been likely to have influenced much of the changes as well.

It was the start of the 1979/80 season. We had just come through the infamous Winter of Discontent. The Labour Party prime minster James Callaghan had just lost power to Margaret Thatcher's Conservative Party, and I had now left Whitehouse Junior School.

Things were changing, and I was heading for what, at the time, was one of the largest secondary schools in the country. Not for the fainthearted, but to be honest it was a great school. I never encountered any trouble from the first day I arrived till the day I signed out five years later in 1984. I believe the media have a lot to do with how people from afar see different areas of Bristol, and unfortunately bad publicity does tend to stick. Maybe others would tell you different stories of their days at school, but we had a pretty tight-knit tutor group who, in the main, all got along and stuck up for one another. It was a time I look back on with pretty fond memories, and can recall some pretty good laughs.

As you can imagine, being a south Bristol school it naturally contained a lot more red than blue. But, surprisingly, there were a number of Gasheads scattered throughout the year groups. Once we got to know each other we would usually stop sometime during the week to discuss the football and what was going on over at Eastville. There was always the odd bit of banter thrown around the classroom but neither side were doing particularly well, so I don't think we could insult each other too much. It was the start of a slide for both clubs that eventually saw City drop to the bottom of Division Four, while Rovers dropped into Division Three. That certainly helped in keeping my City mates quiet for a while, as we had the upper hand for a fair number of seasons.

The 1979/80 season started well enough for Bristol Rovers with a win over Luton Town at Eastville 3–2 on a Tuesday night, which I attended. This was followed up on the Saturday with another victory, this time at home (2–1) against Shrewsbury Town. My memory of the rest of the season is a little patchy, but I do recall a home win against Birmingham City just after Christmas.

Saturday 23 February 1980 was the date of the Bristol Rovers versus Chelsea clash at Eastville Stadium. Bristol Rovers ran out comfortable winners that afternoon 3–0 in front of a decent crowd of 14,176. I can't remember too much about the actual game, but I can recall the violence that took place all afternoon. I was looking forward to the match. Chelsea, even back then, was a big, fashionable club from London, with a good following home and away. When Glen and I arrived and he parked his car there was a feeling that something was brewing, as groups of rival supporters were being ushered around and you could sense that trouble wasn't far away.

Back then police intelligence must have been pretty poor, or maybe they didn't care. Whatever the reason they failed to stop hundreds of rival Chelsea supporters gaining entry into the Bristol Rovers Tote End, which was the home supporters' only section behind the goal.

The Tote End was where we often stood, and you could see there were groups of rival supporters building up in preparation for a brawl.

The Chelsea mob had grouped up near us. You knew it was Chelsea supporters and not the usual crowd of faces that stood there normally. It wasn't too long before a mass brawl kicked off as the two rival groups of supporters fought each other in some fierce fighting.

The police had also arrived in force by now, riding in on horseback, wielding their truncheons, and generally hitting anyone caught in their way. I can't recall any other time I've seen police horses charging around on open terracing at a football match. As the battle intensified it was time to get out of the way. I was only eleven years old so reasonably safe from the trouble – but it was still unnerving, nevertheless. Getting well clear was the best option, as I'm not sure getting trampled on was going to be a good idea.

I was with my brother, and we both walked down the terraces to take up a safer location in the North Enclosure until it calmed down a little. I'm not sure if the steward on the gate did let us into the North Enclosure or if we stood near the gate, ready to get through just in case the situation escalated. The violence didn't stop there, as during the game the Chelsea supporters smashed down a terracing wall at the Muller Road end and continued fighting with both the stewards and the mounted police on duty. Chelsea football supporters were notorious for trouble back then, and I can honestly say it was some of the worst I've ever seen.

The 1980/81 season was one to forget, as Bristol Rovers won only five games all season and were relegated to Division Three. It was also the season when the south stand burnt down, and Rovers had to play a number of fixtures at Ashton Gate. I can say I was at Eastville the last time the south stand ever played host to a Football League game, when Rovers opened the season with a 1–1 draw against Leyton Orient. That evening fire destroyed the structure, and it was never rebuilt. I have since been told by my work colleague Peter Rowe that his younger brother Phillip was the football club mascot at that game with Leyton Orient. It just goes to show what a small world we all live in.

On the plus side it was also the season I saw my first league derby between the two Bristol sides. I'm not really sure I can say I saw much of the game, as I stood on a packed open terrace at Ashton Gate. For the majority of the game I can only recall looking at the backs of the people in front of me, as I struggled to see past all of them. If I said I watched more than ten minutes of that game I would have been lucky, as I jumped, swung, and dodged around the people in front me. The match finished as a 0–0 draw, so I suppose I didn't miss too much. I didn't see many more matches that season.

The following season, 1981/82, Bristol Rovers started life in Division Three with a home match against Chester City. I remember this match not because I was there but because I had gone fishing with a couple of others at Bristol Docks near the old General Hospital. I had taken my pocket-sized radio to keep tabs on any updates as it happened. (Don't ask me if we caught any fish. I haven't a clue.) But I knew the game had finished up at 2–2.

Although I did not attend every match, it was to mark the period that I did go to my very first away game. I had been to Ashton Gate, but you couldn't really consider that as an away game. In fact it was closer than the Rovers home games by some miles. It was to be Newport County on 16 March 1982 at their old Somerton Park ground. The game finished as a 1–1 draw, with Brian Williams netting a penalty for Rovers.

We travelled across the Severn Bridge in Allan's old (sorry, Al) white Mini. I'm sure it had a black leather sunroof that pulled back, but that's another story. And, to be honest, (as I'm much younger than Allan) I am sticking with this version, as he can't recall ever owning such a vehicle.

Let me introduce you to Allan and Kevin Church. Allan is Kev's elder brother, and even now we still attend the majority of Bristol Rovers matches either home or away together. Kev was a mate of my brother Glen, and they all used to drink at the Kings Head on the Bridgwater Road in Bedminster Down. Kev and Glen got to know each other when they were both playing football and skittles together for the pub team. I met Kev when I used to go along to watch their Sunday morning football team, and later, when I was the sticker-up for the pub skittle team, who they played for.

I know it was not the most glamorous football match, but the atmosphere that evening at Newport County had got me wanting more. The pushing and shoving, the singing, and the genuine feeling of being part of a football crowd all caught me hook, line, and sinker, and as a thirteen-year-old, I was in my element. I had arrived on the terraces, and it felt good. If you ever went to Somerton Park and stood on the away banking you would remember that it was basically a sloping bank covered in red gravel. The best way I can describe it is to say it was rather like a speedway track. There would have been good travelling support that evening, as Newport is only a short twenty-five mile or so hop across the Severn Bridge. It was the start of many interesting away trips that were to come over the following seasons on the road with Bristol Rovers.

Chapter Five

A World Cup, Music, and Clobber

The end of the 1981/82 season had seen Rovers finish up the season just below the middle of the table in fifteenth position, and in terms of result highlights during the season it would have to have been the double over our local rivals from BS3. It was the year they also dropped into the basement division after a third successive relegation. That summer of 1982 would also have seen the World Cup taking place in Spain. It was to be the first complete competition that I had watched from start to finish, so España 82 always evokes fond memories.

England had been drawn in Group Four alongside France, Czechoslovakia, and Kuwait. The first game was to be between the two group favourites, England and France. It was an early evening kick-off, so rushing home in time from school wasn't a problem.

England ran out comfortable winners 3–1, with Bryan Robson scoring England's fastest World Cup goal on record to date. The group was won with a 100 per cent record after victories over Czechoslovakia (2–0) and Kuwait (1–0). In the second phase we were grouped with the host country, Spain, and our old footballing foes, West Germany. Both matches were to end in goalless draws, and England ended up eliminated from the tournament without losing a single game. In the five fixtures England had played they won three and drew two, conceding only the one goal in their opening fixture with the French. It was a reasonable record, but not quite good enough to see us into a semi-final.

The West Germans went on to play and beat the French in the semi-finals in an amazing game, which the West Germans won after a penalty shoot-out (does it sound familiar?). The other semi-final was a comfortable 2–0 win for Italy over Poland. West Germany went on to meet Italy in the final, where the Italians ran out 3–1 winners and the evergreen Italian captain Dino Zoff lifted the trophy.

The 1982 World Cup also evokes the memories of an earlier clash in the tournament group stage between Spain and Northern Ireland. Northern Ireland played the host nation, Spain, and nobody had actually given the Irish much of a chance. The Irish were massive underdogs going into the game, but managed to pull off one of the biggest shocks in their history by winning 1–0.

I remember running down from the shower to watch the game on television at home, and switched on the box just as the Irish had scored. I immediately jumped in the air, losing the bath towel from around my waist. It was a moment that I couldn't easily forget, and luckily – as there wasn't anyone else in the room at that time to witness it – I quickly regained my modesty. I enjoyed that tournament but, in my view, the best World Cup tournament was yet to come. That would be England's amazing run in Italia 1990.

The eighties was also a period when a huge casual fashion culture starting hitting the terraces among football club supporters. It is believed that the movement first began up on Merseyside with the boys from Liverpool Football Club back in the late 1970s. This was around the same period when Liverpool ruled both domestic and European football, and their terrace supporters also started to set a fashion style that the rest of football adapted.

As I hit my teens Sergio Tacchini, Fila, Lacoste, and Adidas all started making an appearance around the grounds of England, as did both Harrington jackets and bomber jackets. Stan Smith and the classic Adidas Samba footwear were also the gear to be seen in. It was also a time to ditch those dull black and grey socks for the trendy white fluffy sports socks.

The football terrace music of the day tended to come from the influence of a new Two Tone ska revival, namely from groups such as Madness, The Specials, The Selecter, Bad Manners and The Bodysnatchers. Punk bands were also proving popular, with The Clash, The Damned, Joy Division, the Sex Pistols and U.K. Subs. Personally I preferred the Two Tone sound myself, although I could still jump around to the odd punk sound when the situation required it. Of all the punk bands at that time I would probably have swayed towards Stiff Little Fingers if I had been asked to make a choice.

The first album I remember purchasing was by Madness, with the title *Absolutely*. Mum had just given me some pocket money and it quickly disappeared into the coffers of Asda in Whitchurch, as I became the proud owner of the latest release by the Nutty Boys. I used to play it to death on my small turntable up in my bedroom, when I was supposedly getting on with any homework I had been set earlier in the day from school.

Those albums were quickly followed on the shelf by more Madness releases with the title *The Rise & Fall* and *One Step Beyond...* (which had been released earlier). The album shelf was beginning to fill up around this time, and you could guarantee that come birthdays and Christmas, somebody had added to my growing collection of (mainly modern) ska music. I don't mind admitting now to owning records by Adam and the Ants, Haircut One Hundred, and even Matchbox, as a bit of popular music wasn't all that bad.

There was a time I went Christmas shopping with my sister Debra into town. She asked me to choose an album for a friend of hers, who also liked the ska sound. So I picked the *Two Much Two Tone* album, which had a variety of hits from The Specials, The Selecter, Bad Manners, and Madness, to name a few. To be fair, this album is a pretty good listen even now. Much to my surprise and delight on Christmas morning I unwrapped that very album. It was actually for me all along. I had been tricked.

It was difficult but not impossible to get the odd pair of trendy trainers and a decent polo shirt to show off at the football and, of course, when out with my mates on an evening. Times were hard for everyone during the 1980s. Money was tight for most working families and everyone had to cut back accordingly. I was still at school so had no income apart from my weekly pocket money, which wasn't going to make much of a dent in the cost of new clothes that I was now beginning to crave. I just needed to put on the sincere 'pretty please' routine at home.

'Can I have a new polo, please, Mum?' Or, 'I really need a new pair of trainers, Mum. My old ones are falling apart.' That approach normally worked more often than not, and thankfully I usually got the clothes I felt I needed to feel comfortable at the time on both the terraces and, of course, at school.

My favourite training shoe back then was the three stripes black and white Adidas trainers, with a plain white polo (hopefully a Fred Perry), and a Harrington jacket worn just pushed back off the shoulder. It was a pretty cool look for the thirteen to fourteen-year-old teenage boy at that time. The vintage or retro look, as they have come to call it, has once again grown in popularity.

There was a time I had to make do with a pair of Marlone Marksman trainers, which were almost an exact replica of the Adidas Mundial design. They were pretty cool, really, as nobody even caught on that they weren't the real deal. I also had a blue Pringle jumper in the wardrobe. This tended to be kept especially for Saturday afternoon's football, and was pretty handy when the weather had started to turn cold as well. Glen bought me this one for Christmas one year and I loved it.

Obviously I also needed some decent school clothes and PE kit as well. Luckily (or perhaps not so luckily) our school was pretty weak on following a strict uniform policy, so as long as it resembled something close to blue, black, or white then we all basically got away with wearing what we liked. A tidy pair of shorts and a top were called for during PE so I had a nice pair of white Umbro shorts and a polo shirt to match, finished off with those famous Marlone Marksman training shoes. I remember going along to both school football and rugby trials at one stage looking the part, but disappointingly didn't get a call-up for either.

There was a time during rugby practice when I received an almighty slap across the leg from our PE teacher when he caught me getting a little overly physical in a ruck. I had been told by my brother Glen to make sure that the other kids I was playing against knew I was there. So I went about giving some poor lad a few sharp elbows to his ribs. But it didn't go down too well with the teacher, as he soon let me know. Back then we just took a slap and got on with things. It never did us any harm, and we knew that it would be advisable not to do it again.

I did, however, get a regular place in the inter-tutor group football tournament held every summer term during my time at Hartcliffe School. Hartcliffe School had a few footballers who made it good around the time that I was a pupil there … namely our own Marcus Stewart at Bristol Rovers, who eventually played in the Premiership with Ipswich Town. Marcus was a few school years below me, so I can't say I've played against or with him, but I did play against Graham Underhill, and he went on to play for Bristol City. I believe Graham made his one and only full league appearance against Wolverhampton Wanderers, and had trials at a number of other professional league clubs before playing at a decent non-league level.

I had the honour of representing the school house known as Dundry. There were four houses: Dundry (we played in yellow) Cotswold (red), Mendip (blue), and Quantock (green). The captain of our Dundry team was a friend I still have contact with today, John Allison. John, as I remember him back then, was a fairly tall lad and a pretty good all-round sportsman, who also represented the school at rugby, cricket, and football. He also had the honour of representing the Bristol Boys Schools football team. After leaving school John went for a trial with Somerset CCC, but sadly didn't make the grade.

I'm not sure how we fared over the years, playing for Dundry, but I remember enjoying our time playing football and generally having a good laugh. I haven't got any medals to show for it but it got all of us out of lessons for a few hours, so some good must have come from it.

So the eighties became a decade of a lot of fashion changes and fashion no-nos, as things seemed to be moving pretty quickly throughout this period. Not only were fashion and clothes changing, but there were also some amazing haircuts around, and the contrast between them could be immense. From a simple skinhead cut to a full spike punk cut with a variety of colours to a bleached blonde mullet … there was just no rhyme or reason to it.

There was also a spell during the late 1980s of trackies (shiny tracksuits), but I didn't really go for that look. When I look back now at some of the photographs from that era I'm reasonably happy I didn't sway towards it, either.

As the 1980s went into the 1990s the terrace clobber shifted towards designer named brands such as Aquascutum, Burberry,

Armani, Prada, and Ralph Lauren, but to be honest I think such labels were probably beyond the budget of your everyday football supporter, so there were an awful lot of tacky fakes on show. The clobber seems to be disappearing on the scale it was at during the eighties and nineties now, but it's still on show. If anything terrace fashion is turning full circle, with some of the old classics labels back today, but it is nothing like the scale it once was. There are so much more club and replica shirts worn today than I can ever recall throughout the eighties.

Chapter Six

A Couple of Promotion Close Shaves

Growing up in the early to middle eighties was a good time for me. I loved my football and my music, and I muddled through school life without a care in the world. Bristol Rovers were also slowly putting together a decent side, and became a team that was more often than not there or thereabouts when it came to the promotion shake-up. There were no play-offs back then, or we could have had many more play-off experiences to recall.

The off-field problems at the time over the Eastville Stadium never really came to mind. I wasn't taking much interest in all that kind of politics. I was only just into my teens, and it was all about the football for me at that point. If I heard that we were getting a new stadium then I might lend an ear, but I was happy following my team wherever they happened to be playing. I was only interested in who we were playing that weekend and if I was going to be there, along with how many we were hopefully going to win by.

It was around this time that my brother Glen started to not come along as often as I would have liked, so I started going along to matches with Kev Church. I knew Kev from the football, but I also knew him from the old Sunday morning football days when Glen and Kev had played together in the same team and Glen used to take me along to watch. There was also a time when Kev played skittles up at the Kings Head on Bedminster Down during my time as the team sticker-up, as I think I've already mentioned, so we knew each other reasonably well. Kev was younger than my brother Glen, but was still a few years older than me. So it was great news when Glen asked Kev if he didn't mind me going along with him to the Rovers home games. Kev said he didn't mind picking me up and taking me along, and basically we've been going every week since.

I don't expect I have ever really said 'Thanks' for coming over and picking me up back then, but without it maybe I wouldn't be writing this book today and recalling the many great experiences Rovers have brought us over the years, and maybe I wouldn't have followed Bristol Rovers with as much passion as I have done.

The 1982/83 season started off with a heavy defeat at Brentford, but as the early months progressed Rovers really began to find their feet and started to win a run of games quite comfortably. Plymouth Argyle away at Home Park and then Bradford City at Eastville were beaten 4–0 and 4–1 respectively.

The following week we travelled away to Newport County, expecting our high goalscoring winning run to continue, but we were to become unstuck with a 2–0 defeat. I am pretty sure our visit to Somerton Park on that occasion saw the Rovers fans being relocated into the covered end at the opposite end of the stadium. It certainly generated a lot more noise because we were under cover, but unfortunately we couldn't influence the result that afternoon.

If you have ever had the unpleasant experience of visiting Somerton Park you will remember the awful toilet facilities they had. It was an unlit concrete building, the walls were painted completely black, and the most polite way to describe it was 'A stinking hellhole'. Football supporters were treated like animals back then. Thankfully stadiums have improved beyond recognition nowadays, along with the treatment of travelling fans on the whole. There is still work to be done, but overall it's so much better.

The next few games saw Bristol Rovers hit another goalscoring purple patch beating Wigan Athletic and Millwall 4–0, and then on a Friday evening they took out Leyton Orient 5–1 on their own patch. Rovers followed up these results with more convincing home wins over Reading (3–0), Portsmouth (5–1), and Wrexham (4–0) all before Christmas, as they set out to regain their Second Division status. But, soon after Christmas, Rovers never really got going. We picked up some decent results only to throw away points at vital times, just as we looked to be threatening again.

As the season hit March it was time for my first visit to Elm Park,

Reading. Reading were struggling near the foot of the table, even thought they had the prolific striker Kerry Dixon in their ranks. Rovers's previous visit to Reading the season before had resulted in violence as Bristol Rovers supporters invaded the pitch and fighting broke out with rival Reading fans. The scenes got pretty ugly. It's reported that Rovers fans began ripping up concrete and were trying to hurl lumps into the end occupied by the home supporters, and the game was temporarily held up. I remember being in my dad's car that day and hearing the reports coming through on the car radio as we were heading out to East Street in Bedminster to do a spot of weekend shopping.

So on March 12 1983 I set off with Kev for the relatively short trip up the M4 to Reading. Bristol Rovers had taken a reasonable number of supporters along the motorway, and they made up a sizeable proportion of the overall attendance. I was suitably booted and suited for the day, wearing my straight leg jeans, Adidas trainers, polo shirt, and Harrington jacket, and feeling every bit one of the boys. I was blessed with hair back then, so had a long blonde fringe and a wedge cut.

Reading away was a game I had been looking forward to for a number of weeks. I remember that as the players from both teams went through their prematch warm-up Kerry Dixon took the brunt of the abuse from the Rovers supporters and, to be fair, I recall that he seemed to take it pretty well. As they say, if you're on the end of a bit of stick then you must be a decent player – or at least one who is regarded as a threat. Kerry Dixon was a decent player, which was proved when he went on to play international football for England and had a spell at Chelsea.

We stood directly behind the goal and joined in with the singing of the Bristol Rovers supporters, along with the occasional baiting of the Reading fans. A big terrace song of the day back then was adapted from a cover version in the chart that year sung by Bananarama.

'Na Na Hey Hey Kiss Him Goodbye' had the final line, 'Kiss him goodbye', lyrics replaced with 'Bristol Rovers'. I still smile when I hear it sung today, although it's not as popular as it was back in the 1980s, that's for sure.

It wasn't long before trouble began to break out, as a large number

35

of Bristol Rovers fans had gained entry into the terracing along the side of the pitch reserved only for the home supporters. Fighting broke out between groups of fans before the police were eventually called to try and restore some order, but not before Rovers and Reading had chased each other along the terraces. It was a scene that was happening far too often across the grounds of Britain and it all seemed, sadly, so commonplace. I was never involved in anything personally, but I can say it did give me – as it did a lot of us – a bit of a buzz and excitement watching events unfold, especially as I was just a teenage lad. I suppose I was young and impressionable at that time. When you look back at it now you can see how it was destroying the game.

It was always something to discuss back at school on the Monday morning, especially with your mates and the girls in class who didn't really follow the football like some of us did in school. They all seemed to like listening to the over-elaborated tales of the weekends, or at least I think they did.

One final away trip of that season was to Fellows Park, Walsall, when the Rovers board of directors laid on free coach travel to the game. I travelled up with Kev and Glen on one of the many coaches. In fact a large number of supporters took up the offer that afternoon, and I ended up in a coach alongside the Rovers striker of the time, Graham Withey, which was a bonus. Graham Withey played nineteen games for Rovers during the season, scoring ten goals – which was a decent return, as he was chasing Paul Randall, Archie Stephens, and Nicky Platnauer for his place in the side.

The goodwill gesture backfired as Rovers were hammered 5–0, and we all felt pretty demoralised on the way back to Bristol. It also signalled a bout of food poisoning for Glen, which I can only think came from what looked like a pretty ropy burger van selling fast food at the ground.

Rovers ended up finishing the season in seventh place on seventy-five points. The title was won by Portsmouth, while Cardiff City and Huddersfield Town followed them up in second and third place. Huddersfield Town had a seven-point cushion over us come the end, but it could have been so much closer.

That season's cup fixtures were nothing special as we were knocked out in round two of both the League and the FA cups, losing to First Division Swansea City in the League Cup after briefly threatening a cup upset – and then falling in a replay at Plymouth Argyle in the FA Cup.

I went to Swansea City for the League Cup second leg tie, back during Swansea's first assault as a top-flight club. The Swansea City side, managed by John Toshack, had such names as Bob Latchford, Robbie James, Ray Kennedy and Alan Curtis among the players that they could call upon in what looked a very experienced team, but one that was lacking some youthful additions.

Bristol Rovers had taken a 1–0 lead to the Vetch Field after a great result back in Bristol. The League Cup was still played over two legs during this time, so cup upsets were always a little bit harder to come by as the so-called big boys had two opportunities to put things right if they had slipped up in the first leg match.

Bristol Rovers supporters club had arranged the good old football special train for the second leg tie in Swansea. I boarded the train along with our Glen and both Kev and Allan at the Parson Street train station stop in Bedminster. I can only imagine it was a school half term week, as I'm not sure that I could have persuaded Mum and Dad to allow me to miss an afternoon of school. But, whatever the reason, I was climbing aboard and heading for the Welsh city of Swansea.

It would have been an oxblood Dr Martens away day, as you can never be too careful when crossing the border into Wales. There was normally a welcoming committee at all Welsh clubs in those days. Not that I could have done much as a kid, but it was always better to feel you were prepared for any eventualities.

On arriving at Swansea train station we were met by a small number of the local constabulary, but for whatever reason there didn't seem to be that many. Maybe they were unaware of the numbers that were about to disembark. There was another police escort waiting outside the main station and we set off for the Vetch Field, in what seemed like a never-ending trek across the centre of Swansea.

It had to be one of the most unorganised escorts I can ever remember, as the Rovers supporters were marched along the streets

37

full of early evening commuter traffic. We were walking among the now stationary cars, as they were being held up because of our arrival. It led to the odd wing mirror being snapped back, and the volley of anti-Welsh songs made the locals feel a little uneasy as they sat nervously in their vehicles wondering what was going to happen next (and unable to move).

A group of Swansea City supporters were waiting in small numbers along the route, and welcomed us with the odd token missile being thrown down from the adjoining streets. The sheer number of Rovers supporters was enough to keep any of the Swansea hooligans making a decision to come down and join us, so trouble was kept to a minimum. The result on the pitch was never in doubt, as Swansea City ran out comfortable 3–0 winners on the night and took the tie 3–1 on aggregate.

The return journey back to the station was a relatively quiet walk, due to our defeat. Upon arriving back at the train station a few supporters decided that the odd piece of station furniture and the piles of station flyers needed to be rearranged, as some took out their disappointment of the evening result.

I've recently looked through the programme issued that evening, and Swansea City were advertising a return trip to Paris Saint-Germain for their second leg European cup winner's cup clash for just £30 including a £7 stand ticket. Wow. How times have changed.

The 1983/84 football season was also my last year at Hartcliffe School, and we were to come even closer to promotion by the end of May. But we ultimately missed out again as Oxford United, Wimbledon, and Sheffield United took the three promotion spots on offer.

Football attendances on the whole were generally dropping off around the country, and at Rovers they were following the same pattern. However, they occasionally picked up, as results and performances in general continued to improve in player-manager David Williams's era.

My first away trip that season was to be the trip down to the south coast and a League Cup tie against Bournemouth. Kev was the driver that evening, with Glen and Allan making up the numbers in the car as we set off for our first leg tie. It turned out to be a favourable result as Rovers took a 2–1 victory back home for the second leg, which was a couple of weeks later. It was a game which at one stage I didn't think I was ever going to be allowed in to watch.

The police on the turnstiles that evening decided that I was to be taken to one side and searched and questioned before they were going to consider letting me in the ground. Once they had searched me, checking every pocket, each sleeve – and even my socks – they began questioning me on my name, age, date of birth, address, and school. For some reason they were trying to trip me up with their questions in the hope of getting an arrest, or doing their best to come up with some poor excuse to keep me out of the match.

'If you're telling us lies, boy, you'll spend the evening in the cells' they said. They were just bullying me, to be honest. 'If you're trying to get in as a juvenile, we will find out,' they threatened. I had already explained to them my age and school. I wasn't trying to gain entry as a juvenile. I was a juvenile.

Now that was a case of too much policing … More like police harassment, I reckon. I was fifteen and still at school … Come on, I hadn't even started shaving. If I looked older than twelve back that I would have been surprised. Anyhow I was eventually allowed to enter the ground, once they assessed I wasn't really going to be a threat to the safety of anyone else. Come on … Me at fifteen, seriously? A threat?

The trip back in Kev's white Opel Manta was all smiles, as we sang along to the top tunes of that time that were playing on the radio. I can recall Paul Young was pretty popular, as was his hit 'Wherever I Lay My Hat', and I entertained everyone with my rendition.

I suppose it was a violent time on the streets throughout the eighties, so maybe the police had a massive grudge to bear against the youth of the day. There were the riots of the early 1980s across many of Britain's biggest cities – London, Liverpool, Leeds, Birmingham, and Bristol – along with the regular mass CND marches and of course football violence breaking out every weekend. It was a country in a deep depression as the Conservative Party got to grips with a Britain in what seemed to be an endless downward spiral, with unemployment hitting record highs. The miners' strike and the forthcoming troubles they brought were just months away, and many people could see no end to their hardship and troubles.

Early October was to see a trip to Wimbledon, and what was to become the crazy gang. Rovers were right up in the frame and travelled to London on a run of six wins in their last seven league matches. Rovers came away with a decent 1–1 draw after a goal from Mickey Barrett. June Whitfield of *Terry and June* fame came out on to the pitch at half-time that afternoon, possibility to do a half-time draw or something similar. It's amazing what small details I can come up with at times – I sometimes amaze myself – but I loved my football and I took a lot in. If only I was so enthusiastic now.

I brought up the trip to Wimbledon because it was an eventful journey home. There was no trouble at the match, and I don't recall Rovers having more than a few hundred supporters there, but a bigger game was taking place not far up the road between Fulham and Chelsea. We had followed the Bristol Rovers supporters' club coach out of the ground after the game and off into the streets of London as we found our way back on to the motorway. It seemed a good idea at the time, but we were to get caught up in traffic. And, worse than that, the traffic happened to be Chelsea supporters leaving their fixture at Craven Cottage.

The usual banter was going on as the Bristol Rovers supporters aboard the club coach in front of us exchanged gestures with the passing Chelsea supporters. It wasn't too long until the Chelsea numbers had swollen. The gesturing didn't go down too well with many of the Chelsea fans, and they had begun trying to open up the emergency exit door at the rear of the coach to try and get on board. More and more seemed to arrive on the scene as we sat directly behind the coach wondering what was going to happen next, and of course hoping that we were not about to be identified as Bristol Rovers fans ourselves.

Luckily Rovers are blue and white so I think we would have been able to bluff our way out of it, as long as they didn't pick up on our Bristol accents. The Chelsea fans had by now all but gained entry, as the rear door was flapping open. However, by some miracle the traffic began moving and the coach managed to speed off into the distance leaving the Chelsea supporters taking a step back ... quickly followed by us, feeling pretty relieved.

Next up that season was a trip to Rotherham United on another one of the Bristol Rovers football special trains. We arrived in Rotherham, and as is the custom the local police marched us towards Rotherham's old Millmoor ground. I recall that the locals came out and watched us make our way along their old terraced streets. This had me thinking that I had just been signed up as an extra for *Coronation Street*. There weren't many of us, maybe a hundred, and there was no sign of any disorder as the usual Rovers songs piped up as our arrival was announced. The game finished up as a 2–2 draw with a goal from Ian Holloway and a Brian Williams penalty, which ensured that we didn't return home empty-handed. The trip back was a long trek, but as it was November 5 (Bonfire Night) we were treated to what seemed like our own personal firework display going on outside for the three hours or so journey back into Temple Meads.

The next batch of Bristol Rovers results didn't go too well, as we lost important matches against Lincoln City, Hull City at home, and then away at Oxford United on Boxing Day. I had travelled up to Oxford United's Manor Ground with Kev on one of the official supporter club coaches, but the 3–2 defeat did nothing for either of our Christmases. We had only picked up four points from five games, which knocked back our promotion aspirations.

Results were patchy for the remainder of the season. As soon as we put a decent run together we then reversed all the good work with a couple of defeats and the odd unexpected draw thrown in, which constantly held us back at the wrong times. Going into the last five games of the season we were given no chance, but somehow ended up with a sniff as we played our last game of the season at Hull City. We had won four games on the bounce, and the penultimate game saw us beat Millwall with a late comeback to snatch a 3–2 home victory.

It was to be the last time Mickey Barrett hit the back of the net and the last time many of us saw him in a Rovers shirt, as he was to suddenly and tragically pass away over the summer with an aggressive form of cancer.

We set off on the club supporters' coach for the long journey to Hull City with anticipation of a late promotion but with the realisation it was still pretty unlikely, as a whole set of results needed to go our way. In the end we came away with a 0–0 draw that had also put paid to Hull City's chance of overhauling Sheffield United in third spot, and they were to miss out on promotion by the smallest of margins due to goal difference.

On the final whistle the Hull City supporters didn't take the result too well, and we were bombarded with coins from the adjoining terraces. They got back many of their coins with interest, but I took an executive decision and ended up leaving the ground with a pocket full of coins, as I decided it would be silly to waste them. I must have had enough money to cover my entrance fee by the time I had finished gathering as many coins up as I could fit in my pockets, much to the amusement of Glen, Kev, and Allan. We weren't allowed to leave the stadium for a time, while the small number of police and stewards struggled to keep control of the disappointed Hull City fans. The majority of their force would have been on duty at the nearby Grimsby Town versus Chelsea clash, and it took them a while to get on top of the situation. Chelsea were in the process of wrapping up the Division Two title that afternoon, and it was all hands to the pump at Blundell Park.

There was no cup run to get excited about earlier in the season, as Rovers lost in round two of both the League Cup to Brighton & Hove Albion and, surprisingly, were beaten by (then in Division Four) Bristol City 2–1 in the FA Cup at home. Round one had seen us beat a strong non-league Barnet side 3–1 in a replay after a 0–0 draw at Underhill. The trip to Underhill had seen us leave the pub just before a mob of Tottenham fans were set to join us. A close shave, possibly.

The Football League had also introduced for the first time a cup competition for League Three and Four sides named the Associate Members' Cup, a forerunner to today's Johnstone's Paint Trophy (the Football League Trophy). There was no Wembley final back then and attendances throughout the whole tournament were very poor, as teams and their supporters had yet to take it seriously. Bristol Rovers did manage to make the final, which was played as a one-off match in an away tie at Dean Court against AFC Bournemouth, where we went down 1–0.

Chapter Seven

Calling Time on Eastville

The last couple of seasons at Eastville Stadium before the club moved to Twerton Park in Bath could not have been more different. At the start of the 1984/85 season David Williams was still at the helm as player-manager, and Rovers had a settled squad that were still capable of mounting a serious promotion challenge. Whether the settled squad had been down to the financial situation or down to David Williams believing he still had the right blend of players to mount another promotion assault I'm not sure, but it was going to be our last relative promotion chase for some time to come, as the club were going to hit a very unstable, rocky period both on and off the field.

After the tragic loss of the local favourite Mickey Barrett during the final weeks of the close season, Bristol Rovers were to enter the transfer market and went out and purchased a replacement winger from Queens Park Rangers in the name of Mark O'Connor. Mark O'Connor was to become a firm favourite of mine, as his nimble frame and quick feet provided the Rovers faithful with some entertainment as he orchestrated many opportunities for the Rovers strike trio of Paul Randall, Archie Stephens, and Steve White throughout that first season he was at the club, while also contributing eight goals of his own.

The season had started very well after an opening-day victory at Bolton Wanderers. Next up was a short trip along the M4 to Swindon Town in a League Cup first round first leg tie. Bristol Rovers were to rip Swindon Town apart that day at the County Ground, running out comfortable 5–1 winners, and basically ensuring a passage into the second round of the competition. The journey home on a warm and pleasant sunny August evening was as enjoyable as the result on the pitch, with Rovers fans acknowledging one another as they leant out of car windows, shouting and waving blue and white scarves, and grinning from ear to ear as each car or coach passed. The second leg a week or so later was lost 1–0, but it didn't really matter as Rovers had secured the tie 5–2 on aggregate and were rewarded with a clash against Arsenal, the First Division big boys.

I had just left school during the summer of 1984, and had decided not to stay on at the sixth form but to take up a place at Brunel Technical College at Ashley Down in Bristol. The first leg of the Arsenal tie was going to be on a Tuesday evening, and I really wanted to go and watch Bristol Rovers play one of England's top football clubs and First Division giants Arsenal at their famous North London home, Highbury Stadium. I was only into my second or third week at Brunel Technical College on a block release construction course sponsored by none other than Cowlin Construction, who, later, was to have a big involvement with Rovers.

I did the right thing at the time and asked if I could be given a couple of hours off so that I could go to the match, but to my dismay it was refused point-blank, and I was warned not to go AWOL as it would be reported back to my sponsors, Cowlin.

'Dammit. I will have to call in sick', I thought, but that would have been too obvious – too much of a giveaway – as I had basically already laid my cards on the table and told them I wanted to go to the football. I couldn't risk being kicked off the course or sacked by Cowlin's after only a couple of weeks. Finding a job back in the early 1980s was difficult enough for a sixteen-year-old, and to throw it away so soon wasn't really an option I was willing to take.

At the time I had probably made the correct call, and I went into college on the day of the trip to Arsenal … but maybe in hindsight, all these years later, I wish I had said nothing and just gone off sick for the day. No one would have been any the wiser, and I would have got my game in at Highbury. Sometimes honesty is not the best policy. At the end of the day we only get one chance, so I suppose we have got to do the things we need to do when the time arises, and the time to go to Arsenal for me was back then. It has now been lost forever.

My brother Glen went up with Kev, Allan, and a few others on the train. To say I felt gutted would have been an understatement. Arsenal won the tie 5–1 on aggregate after a comfortable 4–0 win in the first leg, although we did give them something to think about in the home clash as Rovers produced a creditable 1–1 draw. Ray Cashley, the Rovers number one at the time, saved a Charlie Nicholas penalty. Small mercies?.. I suppose that I at least got to see Arsenal in the home encounter.

During my time at Brunel Technical College in Bristol I met up with some good lads, and a few of us still keep in touch. Apart from the serious times of trying to learn a trade we got along pretty well, and had a pretty good laugh. We often spent our lunchtimes playing darts, drinking a beer or two, and snacking on a bowl of chips at either the Ashley Arms or the Foresters Arms. The Ashley Arms has since been totally rebranded, and is now currently known as The Lazy Dog.

It wasn't as if we hadn't already had anything to eat earlier, as we usually walked up the road to fill ourselves with pasties and cakes from the Mounstevens bakery during the majority of our morning breaks. We were also lucky to have the Gloucestershire County Cricket Club right next to our college and they opened up during the summer, so we often could watch an hour of second XI cricket, or grab a game of pool in the Jessops Tavern, which has since long been demolished and turned into an expensive-looking apartment block overlooking the cricket square.

If we weren't up one of the pubs, playing pool, or kicking a ball around on the rear playing field, then it was an opportunity to have a wander over to Mary Carpenter House and catch a few of the girls who were on their hairdressing or catering courses. We arranged to meet the odd one or two on a Friday night in town, but rarely did we ever find them, as we usually ended up on our own mini pub crawls around the Centre and up Park Street.

There was one lecturer at Mary Carpenter House who we used to see on our regular trips there, and he always seemed to be with a group of girl students running alongside him. He always seemed smartly dressed, normally wearing trousers and a waistcoat. He seemed a bit too smooth, so we tended to start singing the Sade chart hit of around that time 'Smooth Operator' to him every time he appeared. I'm not sure he ever cottoned on, but we found it amusing at the time.

46

The majority of us at college were interested in football in one way or another, either playing regularly or (like me) following one of the local teams, so we decided to see if the college staff could get us a game or two arranged. We were lucky enough to manage to get the lecturers to set up a football match with Bath College. We had some tidy players at our disposal but we came up against a side that had obviously been together and trained as a team for a while, as we were soundly beaten. I always fancied myself as a bit of a right back cum left back, but I couldn't do much to prevent our demise that afternoon in front of our small band of supporters made up of college staff and the other lads on our course.

We had a couple of ex-Bristol schoolboy players in our ranks: Kevin Hawkins, who usually played centre half (and had also had a spell with Bristol Rovers as a youngster), and the reliable Billy Bond, who was our goalkeeper. We also had a couple of other tidy players who also played at a decent level around the local league scene. I always say I made Billy look good that day by deliberately handling a cross from one of the Bath players in our box and giving away a penalty just as it looked as if one of them might open the scoring. The Bath lad didn't take it too well, and at one stage I think he was going to take a swing at me before his fellow teammates stepped in.

One of the Bath lads eventually stepped up and fired in a decent-looking penalty, only for Billy to pull off a quality save. He naturally took all the credit, but it was me who gave him the opportunity to be some kind of hero that day.

The next big game for Bristol Rovers that season was the home league clash with a newly relegated Derby County. Derby County were favourites to bounce straight back to the Second Division but found life at the third level not as easy as they would have liked.

I had now begun standing on the North Enclosure at Eastville next to the travelling supporters, and was becoming pretty boisterous with my singing and my baiting of anyone who came visiting the home of Bristol Rovers. Derby brought a good number down that afternoon, so it was to be an entertaining afternoon on the terraces between the two sets of supporters. Rovers continued their great start to the season, winning the game 2–1, and things were looking pretty rosy at this

47

early stage of the season.

The next four games only mustered three draws, and the good start was slowly becoming a distant memory. Next up was a trip South West down the M5 to Plymouth Argyle, and with it also came another 3–2 defeat. To make matters worse we were travelling back home to Bristol in a coach minus a coach window, which had been smashed by a mob of Plymouth fans sometime during the game.

Initially we were advised by the police on duty not to travel back up the motorway with the missing window but the driver made the decision to head back home, as waiting around for a replacement coach could have taken hours. I'm not sure you would be able to do that today, but back then it seemed that health and safety issues were overlooked far more than today. It was early November, so you can imagine how cold that journey would have been. There was always the odd scuffle on our visits to Home Park, as Rovers and Plymouth supporters often fought one another in the open parkland adjacent to the ground.

Unfortunately Bristol Rovers had hit a poor spell just as we were due to play our old rivals from Ashton Gate that season. The clashes between the two sides back throughout the eighties and nineties were something to be savoured, and they were up there alongside the best of football rivalries. They were always tough, competitive matches both on and off the field. It's something that Bristol football has missed in recent years – which is a shame, as they were great events. The build-up and aftermath of a game could go on for weeks.

It would have been an ideal match to bounce back from our poor run of form as derby matches rarely go to form, but we were never at the races and finished up soundly beaten 3–0 in front of what was to be the season's biggest Third Division attendance of 18,672. It wasn't too long before we were able to get our revenge, as the second round FA Cup draw paired us together again at Ashton Gate within a month. Rovers had won 2–1 in a tricky home tie with a plucky little non-league Kings Lynn side who had taken a 1–0 lead that had everyone feeling a bit anxious for a while.

The local media and the red half of the city were half expecting another repeat of the earlier encounter, especially after Bristol City took an early 1–0 lead in the tie. Thankfully Rovers soon responded

48

and bounced back with a majestic display from Paul Randall, and turned it around to hold a 3–1 half-time lead. Rovers steadied the ship and took anything that City tried to throw at them in the second half and, without any more mishaps, finished the game as well-deserved 3–1 winners, and booked their passage into the hat for the third round draw.

The FA Cup tie at Ashton Gate was marred as usual by trouble between the rival sets of supporters, and just after the final whistle my brother was to get hit by one of the hundreds of coins and missiles that were being thrown down from the City fans in the Dolman Stand at the open-end terrace occupied by the thousands of Rovers fans. At first I'm not sure if any of us knew how serious it was, but it ended up with him having a stay at the Bristol Eye Hospital for assessment to ensure that no long-term damage had been suffered. There was another Bristol Rovers supporter in the Eye Hospital at the same time as Glen, who had also been hit by a flying coin thrown from the stands, and his story had been featured on the front pages of the local *Bristol Evening Post* newspaper. Luckily there was no permanent damage done, and my brother was released after a stay of a couple of nights.

The third round draw was to see Rovers drawn out of the hat first to face a home tie against Ipswich Town for a third time in recent FA Cup seasons. It was Ipswich Town who progressed as they got the upper hand and edged a closely fought encounter (2–1) when the match took place the following month. Bristol Rovers briefly picked up their performances throughout December and the early part of January, but the season was soon to fall away after what had been a promising start. Bristol Rovers were to finish up twelve points off of a top three spot, which was filled by Bradford City, Millwall, and Hull City.

There weren't too many highs once January had passed apart from the 1–0 return league victory over Bristol City and my first and only trip to the Baseball Ground, the then home of Derby County. The match finished in an uneventful 0–0 draw but the strange thing about the match was that I later saw that it featured on the kids show *Blue Peter*. One of the presenters on the show at the time was a keen Derby supporter, and had covered the match for the show. It was nice to see us get a bit of airtime for once, even if it was only *Blue Peter*. That's a question for the pub quiz, I reckon.

It wasn't a game that lasted much in the memory, but it was nice to have visited one of Britain's more iconic football grounds from the past. It was home of a few great First Division Championship winning days in the history of Derby County, and where the great manager Brian Clough had made his name. It's sad in a way to see a football ground with a history like the one at the Baseball Ground disappear from football. I suppose the modern day all-seated football stadiums are seen as the way forward and who are we, the paying football fans, to stand in the way of progress?

I can't finish off the 1984/85 season without mentioning the awful events that football was to suffer during the month of May 1985. First we had the tragedy of the Bradford City fire on the final Saturday of the football season, when a fire broke out in the main wooden stand at Valley Parade. Bradford City should have been celebrating a great day, where they would receive the Third Division title. But it will long be remembered in their history as an awful day, in which fifty-six spectators lost their lives and hundreds more were injured.

I had heard about the events at Bradford as I travelled back from the Bristol Rovers game away at Swansea City, and didn't know the full extent of what had happened until I arrived back home. In an almost forgotten tragedy on the same day a young fifteen-year-old supporter was killed by a wall collapsing on him during a riot between Birmingham City and Leeds United fans at St Andrews. Finally we had the Belgium Heysel Stadium disaster before the European Cup Final between Juventus and Liverpool, which resulted in the deaths of thirty-nine (mostly Italian) supporters. A sad month for football, and one we should never forget.

The following season, 1985/86, saw David Williams up sticks and move east to Norwich City, while Bobby Gould was reappointed for a second spell as manager after a short spell managing Coventry City. The club was still going through off-field problems, and discussions on where the team was to eventually end up playing were still hanging over both the team and its supporters. Attendances had started to fall away just when the club could have done with the extra revenue, and things were beginning to look desperate for Rovers. Many of the more experienced names had been shipped off to pastures new as the team took on a completely different look.

It was also to be the season that Gerry Francis signed as a player in what was another one of Bobby Gould's big name captures, which proved to be the pinnacle in Rovers finishing clear of trouble in sixteenth position by the end of the season.

One of the first games to stick out during that season was the trip to Plymouth Argyle at the start of October 1985. I had just decided to take a job at the old Robinson's building in Bedminster in Bristol. It was a stupid idea, really, but when you're seventeen you make mistakes. This was one of mine, so I suppose I can be excused. You could call it a career change, but it ended up more of jumping out of the fire into the frying pan … or a better way of describing it would be to say that I jumped out of the swimming pool into the cesspit.

I had left my sponsorship YTS place with Cowlin Construction, much to the dismay of both my mum and dad, and in hindsight I was a fool. However, I did leave, and by the middle of the following week I had started a new position at a printing firm in Bedminster. It was awful: an early start and a late finish, and the job was the most boring experience of my life. It was not a job for seventeen-year-old lad. You were basically standing all day knocking out preprinted bottle-shaped flyers from big sheets of card. Yawn.

'You'll need to come in on Saturday morning, Craig,' said the boss.

'Sorry, I can't come in this Saturday, I'm off to Plymouth,' I replied.

'You'll come in Saturday and that's final,' he responded.

I didn't say any more but I knew one thing, and that was I wasn't going to be there on Saturday morning. Saturday came and I was off to Plymouth for the match. On looking back it was the right choice, even if we did end up losing 4–2. Nothing was going to stop me watching the Rovers back then, especially some poxy job in a backstreet printers.

Monday morning arrived and I set off for work, only to be greeted by the not so friendly tones of the boss.

'What the f**k do you want? F**k off,' was his morning welcome. What a charming bloke. On returning home, Dad asked me why I was back so early and what had happened.

Dad hit the roof. Not with me, but with how the guy had acted. Dad told me to ring them up and tell them to have my wages ready for the three days I had worked last week.

'OK, Dad,' I replied, and he left for work.

The phone call was met with a similar response from the boss at the printers. As soon as Dad heard about this when he returned home from work later that day he was immediately on the phone.

'We will be down first thing tomorrow morning to collect my son's wages, and you just make sure they are ready,' he told them. 'Well, you just make sure they are there,' I heard him say again. Dad was one of the nicest guys you could ever meet, but he didn't like people treating him or his family disrespectfully.

The following morning we were both at their front door, and Dad was telling the boss a few home truths about how he should and shouldn't be speaking to and treating youngsters. Within a few minutes I had the wage packet in my hand, and we were gone.

It was an awful job and I just hope whoever took over my position got treated better than I did. I can't honestly see how anyone would have wanted to stay there long.

It wasn't too long – no more than a matter of weeks – before I had found another job at a jewellery distribution centre in St Thomas Street near Redcliffe Hill in Bristol. It was mainly a young workforce and we had a great laugh, and although I only stayed about a year I enjoyed my time working there. A few of the other lads working there were also Rovers supporters, so we had plenty in common. We all used to go out at lunchtime playing pool or darts, and often on a Friday a few of us had a drink at the Seven Stars just up the road from where we worked. It wasn't long before long a couple of us had decided to book coach tickets for the Bristol Rovers trip at Chesterfield. History shows that the match never took place, as it was abandoned due to a heavy blanket of fog. It was the thickest fog I had ever seen at a football match. You couldn't see from one end of the pitch to the other, and to be honest we weren't able to see to the end of the penalty box. It really was that thick. Steve White scored for Rovers, but none of us knew we had taken the lead. I recall the news was filtering down from the Chesterfield fans to our left, who began shouting across and telling us that we had scored. It was no surprise to see the game abandoned, as it was really quite farcical.

In all fairness Chesterfield gave us a free ticket for the rearranged game, and Bristol Rovers supporters club offered us all free travel, but we didn't take up the offer. Before the match we tried to get a few beers in a local boozer and it turned out to be fairly comical, as the barman who was serving us supposedly couldn't understand our West Country accents. I know we are Bristolian but seriously it's not that broad, and I'm sure he was just winding us up. We got our drinks in the end, but instead of him trying to be a wise guy he would have been better off checking our ages. I was only seventeen, so it was us having the last laugh. The lad I went up to Chesterfield with was Neil Leech. A long time has passed since then, and after I eventually left that job during 1986 I have never once seen him again.

Strangely enough, Chesterfield Football Club happened to be the last team ever to play a Football League match at Eastville before Rovers were to pack their bags and move out to Twerton Park, the home of Bath City. Saturday 26 April 1986 was to be the last time I stood on the North Enclosure in a small, pitiful crowd at Eastville, as Rovers ended an era with a not very memorable 1–1 draw.

The FA Cup run during the season finished at the fourth round stage but not before we caused a major cup upset, knocking out First Division Leicester City 3–1 at home. The Leicester City side included none other than Russell Osman, who was to spend a short time as manager at Rovers. The fourth round saw a trip to another First Division side, Luton Town, and an opportunity to play on their plastic pitch. Rovers went down 4–0 but we took a huge following that day, and I remember the never-ending snake of Bristol Rovers coaches streaming out of Luton under a police escort.

Police escorts back then seemed pretty cool. It always made you feel important as the police outriders raced ahead, stopping traffic at junctions and roundabouts and ensuring the quickest route out for the club coaches of the travelling supporters.

So that season brought an end to our time at Eastville Stadium in Bristol. Bristol Rovers Football Club and its supporters were about to embark on a new chapter as we followed our team to Bath. It began a ten-year exile from Bristol. The Bath City Twerton Park years were upon us, and nobody knew exactly what lay in store, or if we would even have a football club to support for much longer.

Our Dad (seated) with Glen (standing) my sister Debra and me on my bike
(minus the Bristol Rovers scarf... Summer 1976)

Dad at Wembley in front of the twin towers

Bristol Rovers at Torquay United (2013)

Rovers supporters invade the pitch at Wycombe Wanderers (2014)

Bristol Rovers Football Club Memorial Stadium

Around 3,000 Rovers supporters at Fratton Park Portsmouth (2016)

Glen and me outside Wembley before Bristol Rovers Conference Play-off
Final victory over Grimsby Town (2015)

Inside Wembley as Bristol Rovers and Grimsby Town line up for the start of the Football Conference play-off Final which we went on to win after a tense penalty shoot-out (2015)

Inside Wembley Stadium

Promotion back to the Football league after just one season away

Me and my Nephew Wayne Ford in the Hilton Sky bar Wembley (2015)

Me with Irene the Gorilla

Pre-season encounter for Bristol Rovers at the Memorial Stadium v Arsenal U21's

Viewed from the Grandstand (2015)

Mum wearing my blue & White quarters early 90's

Bristol Rovers supporters after promotion from League Two May 2016

Another tense afternoon saw us clinch promotion in the 92th minute with a Lee Brown winner and a 2-1 victory over Dagenham & Redbridge

Nephew Wayne (second Left) and Brother Glen (3rd Left) with a couple of mates outside the Queen Vic on Gloucester Road Bristol celebrating Bristol Rovers back to back promotions (May 2016)

Chapter Eight

Exile in Bath

The club started its ten-year exile (in the hope of saving the club from extinction) in the city of Bath as the 1986/87 season kicked off. It was to be was a massive gamble. So how many supporters were actually going to follow a Bristol team when its ground was fifteen or so miles away from Eastville in a different city, and at a fairly uninspiring non-league ground? The attendances took a further knock at first, and the football on show wasn't much to shout about as the football club struggled to hold on to their Third Division league status.

But under the guidance of Bobby Gould, along with a few experienced heads, a loan player added here and there for good measure, and the eager young pretender, survival was achieved. Just. The Twerton Park pitch took a bit of stick during that first season, as you only had to spit on it and a game seemed to be cancelled.

Nick Tanner and John Scales lined up for Rovers in our first season in exile, and both players went on to play regularly for Liverpool's first team in the Premiership … as did Gary Penrice, who was also part of the Bristol Rovers initial squad back then. He eventually left a couple of years later for a career in the Premiership with Watford, Aston Villa, and Queens Park Rangers.

Bobby Gould, in what was good old Bobby Gould style, brought in the evergreen player Kenny Hibbitt. And, to be fair, every player Bobby signed over the years who was seemly coming to the end of his career played his part during his time in the blue and white quarters.

There was little to remember during the 1986/87 season but I made the long trek over to Bath with Kev and, to be fair, we both watched the majority of home matches that season, as did Allan. There was a time that Kev's car broke down near the Hicks Gate roundabout on our way to one of the early matches at Twerton Park. I can't remember the exact game, or season, but we ended up hitching a lift with some fellow Rovers supporters as we walked along the Keynsham bypass making our way towards Bath. Nothing was going to stop us watching Rovers back then. There wasn't the luxury of mobile phones at the time, so it was just a case of getting on with it if we were going to get to the match.

We usually had a few beers before the game at the Old Crown on Twerton high street, and this was normally the establishment where we met up with Allan and any of the other guys who were going to the match. The Old Crown was a small pub and was always jam-packed with Rovers supporters, so occasionally we had to drink at the Full Moon, which was a much larger pub and just as busy, but at least you could move around a little easier. I can't recall ever seeing large groups of supporters from the travelling teams come into these pubs. Where they used to drink I haven't a clue.

The highlights of the season were mainly to come in the local derbies. We travelled up to Swindon Town on a Tuesday night in November 1986 and returned home with a surprise 2–1 victory, and on New Year's Day we defeated Bristol City at Ashton Gate 1–0 with a storming long-range effort from Gary Smart with less than five minutes remaining. The ball hit the net right in front of the masses of travelling Gasheads, and I remember celebrating that one as if we just won the league. It was all hands to the pump that day, and we even had to overcome the loss of our goalkeeper Tim Carter to injury, as we ended up playing the outfield player David Mehew between the sticks for the final fifteen minutes or so of the match.

The season ended up with Rovers playing seven of the final ten league games at home due to all the postponements throughout the season. We lost the majority, and went into the final league match requiring a point away to guarantee our survival in Division Three.

The final match saw us travelling the short distance across the Severn Bridge to take on Newport County at Somerton Park. The poor run of results left Rovers in a spot of bother, sitting a little too close to the bottom of the table to feel comfortable. Bolton Wanderers were closest to us in twenty-first place, and we were just three points better

71

off than them in twentieth. It was possible that we would fall through the Third Division trapdoor and into the fourth tier if a number of results were to go against us and we suffered another defeat. It could get close, so we really needed to get a result and keep our own fate in our own hands.

Kev, Allan, and I set off, and we arrived in Newport just as the pubs were filling up with hordes of travelling Rovers supporters. Kev had arranged to see a few lads we knew, and it wasn't long before we were all having a few beers and discussing the afternoon ahead. It was surprising how many Bristol Rovers supporters actually came from south Bristol, which is basically the Bristol City supporter's heartland. Over the coming years I got to know a fair few of them and we all often travelled to away matches either in hired minibuses on trains or even in the back of transit vans, which was never the most comfortable way to travel.

The minibus started its journey from Withywood, and picked supporters up in Hartcliffe, Bishopsworth, Highridge, and Bedminster Down. They were a pretty sound bunch of lads, to be honest, who enjoyed their football, a few beers, and the general shenanigans that went with it. None of them were troublemakers, but could all pretty much look after themselves and one another if the need were to arise. We all had a few laughs over the years travelling up and down the country watching our favourite team.

Bristol versus the Welsh, especially the South Welsh football clubs, were the next best thing after a Bristol Rovers v. Bristol City derby clash, and it wasn't unusual to see the odd outbreak of violence between the various groups of supporters. Newport County away had the potential of being one of those occasions, but not quite on the scale of a Cardiff City or Swansea City.

After spending a few hours in the early May sunshine drinking a few beers and singing a few songs it was time to head off to the ground, and hopefully pick up the result we desperately needed. We must have been reasonably close to the ground when we were met by a group of Newport fans, who were clearly looking for a target to hit. They were all casually dressed, and looked every bit the part of a football hooligan. There were around twenty of them, who suddenly appeared in front of us as we rounded the corner.

72

Now, as far as I can remember, it was just me and Tony. Tony was from Withywood, and in his early to mid-twenties. He was a friendly lad who was easy to get on with, and normally pretty much level-headed. He was so level-headed that he picked up the nickname from our group of 'Captain Sensible'. The Newport boys clearly thought their Christmases had come all at once with an isolated couple of Bristol Rovers fans but they had not banked on what was about to happen, as Tony took the initiative with his approach and started moving towards them. This immediately struck doubt in the minds of the group of Newport boys.

'Come on, then. Come on,' they said.

'Yeah, who wants it?' Tony yelled, along with other words that weren't as pleasant. It was enough to have them reconsidering their options, and clearly they weren't sure about making the first move. I wasn't saying a word, just scanning the group and looking out for anyone likely to make a move on us, and all the time staying pretty close to Tony, as his aggressive approach was clearly working.

It soon became obvious that they weren't really up for the confrontation they were looking for, even if the odds were stacked in their favour. Kev is adamant that he and a few others were close behind. However, at the time all I could see was a situation with massive odds against Tony and me, and one that might have taken a fair bit of fighting to get out of. Kev and the rest must have been in sight as the Newport boys were soon on their heels making a hasty retreat, although I like to tell the story of how it was just the two of us who turned a mob of baying Newport fans.

I haven't seen Tony for a number of years now, but I know Kev still sees him around occasionally. Strangely enough I do see his brother-in-law Nick on and off when I'm out for a beer, and I always have a chat to ask how he's getting along. He now spends most weekends travelling up to watch Manchester City and doesn't really bother with Rovers any more, which is a shame. Tony was a good 'un.

The usual heavy-handed South Wales police greeted us at the turnstiles and checked that nobody was trying to sneak anything illegal into the ground. It was the norm back then, so it wasn't anything new to any of us. I remember watching the police make one

73

lad remove his Dr Martens oxblood boots on a previous trip to Newport. He must have been wearing the maximum number of eyelets, as he was there for quite a time undoing his laces as I queued at the turnstiles.

Once in the ground the serious business of ensuring that we got at least a point from the game was about to begin. The away fans were now under cover and, as I mentioned before, it led to a noisy atmosphere from the Rovers contingent. Much to the relief of the travelling support Phil Purnell popped up to hit the Rovers winner, and the worry and embarrassment of relegation was avoided.

As the final whistle approached it was obvious that a number of Rovers fans were planning a pitch invasion. Now I'm not sure if it was a pitch invasion to celebrate the sheer relief of staying up or not, but my intention was to catch up with Geoff Twentyman Jr., the Rovers defender, and ask him for his shirt. Geoff Twentyman Jr. is the son of Geoff Twentyman senior the ex-Liverpool footballer and chief scout who sadly passed away in February 2004. It was still back in the good old days of high-security perimeter fencing, which penned us all in like cattle, so there was a bit of climbing to be negotiated first before I could put my plans into operation.

On hearing the final whistle I was up on the fence and setting off along with around thirty or so other Rovers fans. I knew Kev was over but I can't recall anyone else, as I was on a mission sprinting after Twentyman. Unfortunately the Rovers invasion quickly sparked a similar but smaller number of Newport fans and a number of police as well, which quickly had the players from both sides making for a quicker than expected exit and disappearing down into the safety of the tunnel.

I had now reached the middle of the pitch and was watching Geoff Twentyman Jr. becoming a far and distant conquest, and the chance of his shirt was quickly vanishing. The police now had sufficient numbers to surround us, and proceeded to escort us back into the visitor's enclosure to join the rest of the Rovers supporters.

So Newport became a fairly eventful day both on and off the pitch: a local Severnside derby, the right result, and a short dash across the Somerton Park pitch to finish it off. Bristol Rovers finished up in nineteenth position on fifty-one points. In the end they were six points clear of Bolton Wanderers, who failed to win their final game that afternoon. They were the team that was eventually relegated after a divisional play-off. It was to be the last time Rovers played Newport County in a league match for some twenty-six years, and it finished off the first season in exile in Bath for Bristol Rovers.

Chapter Nine

Rovers on the Road

Remarkably, the time that Bristol Rovers spent at Twerton Park Bath brought the club a spell that nobody could have imagined, especially after their first season in exile during the 1986/87 season saw the football club survive after a last-day victory at Newport County. A defeat that day could have seen Rovers drop into the Fourth Division for the first time in their history and, with the club in peril as it was, who knows what might have happened?

Bobby Gould, the manager at the time, was tempted away from the club for a third time after his short, two-year spell as manager. He was replaced by ex-England international footballer Gerry Francis, whose only previous managerial spell had ended in the sack at Exeter City. Gerry Francis was already a familiar face at the Gas, as he had had a few games as a player under his belt with the club when he came to the end of a long and illustrious playing career. Francis would have been aware of the club's difficult plight, so would have taken on the manager's role with his eyes wide open to the current situation. His appointment was to be an inspired choice. He was to change the football club around, and brought back pride to the club and its supporters.

Gerry Francis bonded the players he already had, made some astute signings, gave the team belief, and also gave the supporters something to be proud of, as he put together a team made up mostly of keen non-league signings with a point to prove.

It was also to be a spell which saw many away trips for me and our group, as we spent many Saturdays travelling up and down the motorways of Britain following our beloved Bristol Rovers and encountering a story or two along the way. Blackpool was to become a regular trip for us over the next few seasons. It was to be the venue of the most memorable day as Bristol Rovers supporters when we clinched the Third Division Championship as the end of the 1989/90 season.

My first trip north to Blackpool would have been almost three years earlier during the first season with Gerry Francis in charge in the month of August 1987. There was nothing too memorable in the result that August bank holiday, as Rovers fell to a 2–1 defeat. We travelled up in a posh-looking minibus hired from Hareclive Road Car and Van Rental, who were based on the Hareclive Road in Hartcliffe. The company name and petrol station where it was operated from have long since gone, and is now a block of terraced houses.

I'm not sure who drove that day, but I do recall a number of off-licence stops to stock up on beer and spirits before we had even left Bristol to keep everyone refreshed during the journey north. There was one member of our posse that day who thought it would be a good idea to take back a bunch of flowers for his missus to help smooth things over when he returned home later that evening, I'm not 100 per cent sure he actually purchased them … but it's the thought that counts, so they say, isn't it?

Most of us had consumed the odd can or two by the time we reached Blackpool. Some had consumed a lot more than others, so a few were already a little worse for wear. But who cares? I think you need a drink or two to take away the pain of watching the football sometimes.

I'm pretty sure it was on this trip that a local Blackpool lad somehow latched on to our group and, for whatever reason; he decided to become our unofficial pub and working men's club tour guide. It seemed a little weird at first, and a few of us questioned his motives, as we wondered if he was actually leading into some kind of Blackpool mob ambush. He wasn't, and he turned out to be genuine. Where he appeared from and where he disappeared, I'm not sure anyone knew, as once we headed for the game he was gone. It was very reminiscent of 'Camouflage', the Stan Ridgway song from around that time. Maybe he was just out to do a good turn.

Saying that we all headed for the game wasn't entirely correct, as a few of the lads couldn't be bothered to leave the pub and spent the afternoon drinking and playing cards. The trip back home to Bristol after the match was as entertaining, as always, with the odd beer stop en route. The number of times one of us used to get sprayed by a fizzed-up can of beer was no odds to anyone.

The next away game was only a few weeks away, and we had the good old local derbies to look forward to back then. The short trip down to Bristol City's home, Ashton Gate, wasn't far enough to think about hiring vans, so most of us met up in the ground. That afternoon was no different to any other local derby back at that time: the games were always fiercely contested and hostile, full-blooded affairs. The number of coins and missiles that used to be thrown down from the Dolman Stand into the open end where the Bristol Rovers supporters were packed into had to be seen to be believed. You always had to make sure you had one eye on the game and one on the stands, as you never knew what was going to be coming your way next.

As I mentioned earlier, my brother Glen took a coin in the eye at one of these games and spent a couple of days being monitored in the Bristol Eye Hospital. It was still the days when both sides competed in the Gloucestershire Cup final, so local derbies were a regular occurrence. The Gloucestershire Cup was never as well-supported as a league encounter – but nevertheless some could turn into tasty affairs on occasions, especially if they were held just before the start of a new season.

The FA Cup that season saw us drawn away to non-league opposition and a trip to VS Rugby. I can't remember anything good about this trip. My lingering memory is of playing at a ground that resembled a park more than a stadium. The terracing, as I recall, was virtually non-existent, and it was basically all on one level. Rovers needed a replay after struggling to a 1–1 draw that day. The game was played in what seemed like near darkness as the floodlights were awful, as was trying to find your way out of the ground and across a large, open and unlit scrubland next to their ground and back to our transport after the game. I was glad to get away from that place and wouldn't have fancied returning, but it was to be another ground ticked off as visited over the years.

As the season progressed there were glimpses of what was to come as Bristol Rovers pulled off some impressive results and put together a decent finish to the season. A 4–0 victory over high-flying and eventual champions Sunderland on a Tuesday evening at Twerton Park was probably the highlight of a highly entertaining second half to the season. Unfortunately it also marked what was to be the end of the playing career of our veteran midfielder Kenny Hibbitt, after he was on the end of a rash challenge from an extremely frustrated Sunderland player. The last two fixtures of the season saw Rovers run out comfortable 3–0 home winners against promotion-chasing Walsall before travelling to another promotion-chasing side, Brighton & Hove Albion, at the Goldstone Ground.

Brighton was to be our final destination of the season, and the usual crowd boarded our hired minibus and headed towards the south coast. Brighton needed to win to ensure their promotion back up into the second tier of English football, and a large crowd of over 20,000 was expected to be there to witness it.

After picking us all up and stocking up on beer, as was customary for our away trips, we soon reached the M4 motorway and were heading for the south towards Brighton. Nobody gave it a second thought that the final Saturday of the football season was also the weekend of the popular Badminton Horse Trials and that the traffic around the motorway junctions near Bath were going to be busy. We were all soon to discover that, and by that time a few too many cans had been consumed. Normally it wouldn't have been a problem: just a quick service station stop en route and everyone would be happy.

It was not the case that day, as we were soon grinding to a halt and moving at a snail's pace as the traffic built up. The majority of us were now just about bursting for a pee, and when you're stuck somewhere unable to go anywhere then it always seems so much worse. We were all but stuck in the middle lane on the M4 motorway, and this wasn't an ideal place to be when you were desperately in need of a pee. Thankfully there were plenty of empty cans and a couple of plastic cider bottles lying around, which needed to be put to good use. As the bottle was passed around the back of the minibus a number of us took our turn to fill it up before it was duly emptied out of the sliding window of the minibus.

As the minibus moved along it was obvious that the wind was going to catch a certain amount of the contents of the bottle as it was being emptied out and the unfortunate ones, which included me, had the occasional unpleasant shower to deal with. It's amazing how quickly you can fill a bottle up, so as you can imagine the rear footwell of the minibus was soon becoming an open urinal. What the passing motorists heading towards Badminton made of us and what was going on God only knows.

As the traffic began moving a bit more quickly we passed a coachload of what looked like sixth form schoolgirls heading off to the horse trials waving out at us, so we returned the favour to be polite. As we eventually started moving a bit quicker and disappeared off into the distance a couple of the lads on board our minibus sent them on their way by mooning at them in a friendly way out of the side window, much to their and our amusement. After we had a refreshment stop later on the journey in a posh boozer en route we eventually arrived in Brighton with little time to spare before the match was due to kick off.

It was impossible to park anywhere. All the streets were packed with cars, and any spaces that were available had double yellow lines covering them. Sod it. We ended up leaving the van parked on a grass verge and we all bundled out and headed towards the ground. A police motorbike rode by and told us to move the minibus or we would get a ticket. Nobody took any notice, and on our return we had our parking ticket, as he had promised. I'm not sure if we had a whip-round on the way home to all chip in to pay the ticket or not. To be honest, some of the whip-rounds that went on over the years could be rather dubious. Who walks round the carriage of a train and collects for the driver? Yep, I've seen it done on a Rovers away day, and loads of people on board were actually chucking in their loose change.

Brighton achieved their promotion that afternoon as they beat us 2–1, but not before we gave them something to think about before the final whistle eventually confirmed their victory. The vast majority of the Brighton supporters were just enjoying their day, but we still had a few who pelted us at the end of the match with coins – many of which were soon being thrown back, as I had gone past collecting them up by that time. So another season was done and dusted. We all went away that summer with a little more belief, and the following season was to produce further improvement on the pitch.

The 1988/89 season was to finish with Bristol Rovers reaching the play-off final even though it ultimately ended in a 2–1 aggregate defeat over two legs against Port Vale. I clearly remember sitting on steps of the terracing after the final whistle had blown at Vale Park feeling absolutely gutted that we had come so close to what would have been the first promotion I would have experienced as a Bristol Rovers supporter. There is nothing like the feeling you get for your own team. Nothing compares to it. The joys of winning or the hurt in defeat are unrivalled.

Thankfully, twelve months down the line from that play-off defeat at Vale Park we would all be celebrating and feeling the exact opposite to that day, as we won the Third Division Championship. And we also had our first-ever trip to the famous twin towers of Wembley Stadium to look forward to, as we had also reached the final of the Leyland Daf Cup. The highlight was undoubtedly the final day of the 1989/90 season and the trip to Bloomfield Park, Blackpool, where we were crowned champions. It was the first promotion I had experienced. It felt amazing, and I was going to enjoy it. Promotion had been achieved three days earlier at a bouncing Twerton Park as we comfortably beat our fierce rivals and then title challengers Bristol City 3–0. A Devon White double and a penalty from Ian Holloway wrapped up our promotion that evening and put the outcome of the title in our hands. If we were to win the final game of the season at Blackpool on the Saturday then the title would also be ours.

The achievement had been amazing as Rovers were commonly known in the press as 'Ragbag Rovers', due to the club being without a home of their own, playing outside of Bristol, and training at a chocolate factory in Keynsham. Even some of the club offices were run from Portakabins on the factory site. Rovers also lost two of the club's most influential players during the season, as Nigel Martyn left to become Britain's first £1 million goalkeeper when he was transferred to Crystal Palace and Gary Penrice left for Watford in a £500,000 deal. It was a credit to manager Gerry Francis, his staff, and of course the players he had assembled, that they finished the season as they did.

If we had travelled to any away league games during that season then I'm afraid they have all been erased from my memory, as nothing could compare with the memories of that last-day victory at Blackpool on 5 May 1990.

Saturday 5 May 1990 was a sunny day, as I remember it, when we set off early in the morning from Bristol on our trek north to Blackpool. Football matches back then, especially the final few games of a football season, always seemed to be scorchers. Maybe they were, or maybe that's just how I remember them. Winter seemed cold, with snow, and summer seemed hot and sunny.

Kev Church was the driver that day. He had recently started a new job,and as part of the job he had the use of a transit van. I'm not sure he had actually been given permission to transport a dozen or so twenty-year-old Rovers fans on a drink-fuelled promotion party to Blackpool, but nevertheless it was our transport for the day. The usual suspects were on board, the same guys who we had been travelling to away games with already, along with my brother Glen, who rarely went to home or away matches back then as he had recently married and had young children to care for.

And there was Jeff Wherlock, a friend from where I worked. Jeff had only just started taking an interest in football. We were soon to become good buddies and he had decided to come along with us, which was his first-ever Bristol Rovers away match as a newly installed Gashead to our ranks. It was to be an eye-opening introduction to following Rovers, and one which couldn't have been better picked as your first match day experience.

Jeff arrived over at my parents' house on the morning of the game carrying a plastic bag of supplies for the day ahead.

'What have you got in the bag, Jeff?' I enquired. He picked up the bag and proceeded to show me what he had brought along. There were a couple of packets of crisps, a bar of chocolate or two, and he then revealed a large bottle of dandelion and burdock.

'Oh, shit,' I said. 'You can't take that, Jeff. You'll have the piss taken out of you all day. You're going to have to leave that here'.

There was no way he could have taken that along. What an

82

introduction that would have been. He would have never lived it down, especially at it was his first trip with the other lads. Thankfully Jeff took my advice and left it behind.

Once Kev had picked us all up and the van was stacked with beer and spirits it was time to get on the road and make tracks for Blackpool. It wasn't too long before the beer was disappearing, and one of the guys named Winnie had already finished off a bottle of sherry. Now a whole bottle of sherry isn't the easiest fortified wine to drink in around an hour on your own but, along with necking a few cans of lager, he had managed it by himself – and all this before reaching Cheltenham.

We were soon stopping off en route somewhere around the West Midlands for a comfort break, while some of the others needed to top up on the their lager supplies as they were running low. When we had almost all got back in the van Winnie came running across jumping in the van carrying a full box of unopened chocolate dips, which he had acquired from outside the service station. They must have just been delivered and had yet to be taken inside the shop. We all just doubled up with laughter. The day was turning out to be one of the best road trips we had had together, and as long as we won on the pitch later that afternoon it wasn't going to be beaten for a long time.

Once the doors of the van were shut some of us were soon enjoying a chocolate dip to go with our beer. Winnie soon decided that not only were the chocolate dips for eating, but maybe they would also look good as a face paint in the style of the eighties pop group Adam and the Ants. Within half an hour or so we were aware that the police had started following us, and it was only a matter of time before the blue flashing lights lit up and we were being beckoned to pull over on the hard shoulder of the motorway.

The chocolate chips were quickly hidden, as were the many empty beer cans and bottles. One of the coppers walked up to Kev, who was driving. He asked him to get out of the van and started questioning him, while the other came around the back and opened up the rear doors. Most of us had opened cans and had quickly hidden them behind us out of sight. The van, luckily, was full of clean and used hand towel rolls (the ones that are fitted in public toilets at pubs and clubs and the like), and they did a great job of not only concealing everything but also of soaking up the beer that was now flowing from the opened cans of beer which had fallen over in our haste to hide them.

Jeff was sitting next to me and you could see that he was doing a great impression of a sponge soaking up the beer through his jeans, which made it pretty difficult to keep a serious face. I was itching to just burst out laughing. It had crossed my mind that the chocolate dip saga was the reason why we had been pulled over, but thankfully that was not the case. To have been carted off for the afternoon to the local nick and miss out on the Rovers promotion party would have been a nightmare.

Kev was still up at the front having the third degree from Mr Plod. By all accounts we had been reported by a few motorists travelling northwards saying they had seen the side door being opened and closed with a van full of lads inside, so they had just been acting upon that. The copper talking to us at the rear asked if we had been drinking. Pretty obvious, really. I expect the van was stinking like a brewery.

'No, just the odd one,' came a reply. The other copper had now finished talking to Kev and had come around and opened up the sliding side door. With that a half a dozen or so empty beer cans went tumbling out on to the hard shoulder of the motorway. This wasn't going well for us.

'And what's that on your face?' asked the plod, who had noticed the smeared chocolate across Winnie's face.

'Chocolate sweat,' Winnie replied. The plod just shook his head and, thankfully, left it at that.

We were told in no uncertain terms to clear off out of their patch, and watch our step. If they heard any more reports about us then we would be pulled over and stopped from travelling any further. They also would be notifying the next force of us travelling, so we were to watch ourselves. Kev was also told that the company he worked for would be receiving a call about what had happened. Kev didn't work there that much longer. He was called in the office the following week to explain what had been going on that weekend.

We arrived in Blackpool without any more mishaps. We were

lucky that the two coppers on duty that day didn't want a morning of paperwork, which they would have had if they had brought us all in. I expect they were just coming to the end of their shift, if the truth was known, and they wanted to get off on time.

Blackpool was a sea of blue and white. There were Rovers supporters everywhere, many making a weekend of it and either arriving the night before or staying on until the Sunday. The atmosphere was already well in the party mood. The Gas were there to party, there was no doubt about that. Once parked we took in a few of the local pubs before ending up in what can only been explained as a lively city centre nightclub in the early hours of a Saturday night … but now it was still early afternoon. Music, dancing, flashing disco lights, and half-wasted girls: it certainly had it all. The place was buzzing, and was packed out. If Bristol Rovers weren't going to score that afternoon then I'm sure a few of us could have quite easily.

The game went perfectly, as Rovers ran out comfortable 3–0 winners against a Blackpool side who were facing relegation to the bottom tier of English football. The Third Division title was ours: it belonged to Bristol Rovers. My team was finishing as champions. The travelling support we had taken that afternoon had to be seen to be appreciated. We had taken over more than half the ground, and the sheer numbers there that afternoon was amazing.

As the game reached the last ten minutes large numbers of Rovers supporters were beginning to climb over the fences, and had started to surround the playing surface as we all made our way closer to the pitch in anticipation of the final whistle and the eventual mass pitch invasion to join the celebrations. Paul Nixon, the Bristol Rovers New Zealand international, smashed home the third goal into the keeper's top left-hand corner just before the final whistle, which immediately sparked an earlier than expected pitch invasion – which held up the game for a few minutes, as hundreds of supporters were sent back off the playing surface to all four corners of Bloomfield Park. Eventually the game got back under way before the final whistle did finally blow, and the supporters jubilantly stormed on again to celebrate. I'm not sure where everyone ended up but I ran on and made it to the end of the penalty area, where I hoisted up Glen on to my shoulders and watched and joined in the singing with thousands of happy Rovers supporters. At last my team had achieved promotion, and it felt pretty good. I can't remember the journey back but boy, it would have been one of great celebration, that's for sure.

The season wasn't over yet, as there was a small matter of our first-ever Wembley appearance to soak up and enjoy a few weeks later. It was a trip that ended in a 2–1 defeat to Tranmere Rovers, but the event far outweighed the result that day, and the main goal of promotion had already been safely secured.

I travelled up with my dad that afternoon on an organised coach from Whitchurch. I didn't bother travelling with the minibus lads that day as I didn't think it was really going to be our dad's scene, to be fair. I can still look back on it with fond memories. Dad didn't go to many matches, as I've mentioned before, but to be with him on Bristol Rovers's first-ever Wembley trip was special, and I'm pleased we were together that day.

The start of the 1990/91 season was eagerly awaited as it was going to be great to be playing the likes of Leicester City, Newcastle United, Ipswich Town, West Brom, Middlesboro, Wolverhampton Wanderers … the list just went on and on.

Before the start of the new season we had a World Cup summer to enjoy. Italy 1990 will always go down as my favourite World Cup tournament ever. I was still at Brunel Technical College back in 1990 so it was generally the main discussion every day when we arrived for morning lectures. England reached the semi-finals and eventually lost to West Germany (as they were known back then) on the dreaded penalty shoot-out. I still argue today that we were the best side in the world at that time, and if 1966 was ever going to be repeated then that would have been the year.

So 1990/91 saw us back in Division Two, the equivalent of today's Football League Championship, and our first fixture was away to Leicester City. Replica blue England shirt on and ticket in hand, we all were off again and travelling to Leicester. Bristol Rovers were back on the road. Rovers lost that first game 3–2 but put in a brave performance and more than held their own during the first season back in Division Two, finishing in thirteenth place.

There were some great venues to visit that season and over the next few seasons, to be fair, and I thoroughly enjoyed the ones I took in during that period. A great 2–0 win at Swindon Town and the trip to West Brom both stick in the mind from the first season back in Division Two, along with that opening day trip to Leicester City. Although we lost the match at West Brom we got chatting to some good lads from West Brom in a pub before the game, and they even introduced us to Don Goodman as he came in for a prematch beer. Don Goodman was a forward at West Brom, and out injured at the time.

The following summer Gerry Francis left to become manager of Queens Park Rangers, and he took a few of our players with him. In return a couple joined us from QPR, but the team never quite reached the same heights as it did under Francis.

Martin Dobson was appointed manager in his place, and was quickly shown the door after a bad start to the season. We still finished up the season in a mid-table position of thirteenth under manager Dennis Rofe, and we had some great home results over the big spenders in the division. Kenny Dalglish brought his Blackburn Rovers side to Twerton Park and was sent packing as Bristol Rovers ran out 3–0 winners in one of the most memorable matches that season.

The emerging teenage star Marcus Stewart kept us going that year, and it looked as if Dennis Rofe might be able to emulate the success of Gerry Francis. However he was eventually ousted by the appointment of Malcolm Allison the following season, before John Ward made his first appearance as manager and steadied the ship for a few seasons (albeit not before we had been relegated back to the third tier at the end of 1992/1993).

Over the next few seasons our away minibus trips were becoming fewer and fewer, and if we did go to an away match it was usually me, Kev, and Allan Church, and now Jeff Wherlock, making the trips together. I suppose everyone was getting older, families were coming along, and fewer of us could go to matches all the time. I'm not saying we still didn't have a few laughs, but it wasn't on the same scale. There were still times at Blackpool where we had rides on the trams, a quick visit around the pleasure beach, or the day I came back with a garden gnome after buying him before a game and taking him to the football. If we didn't drive to matches then there were still a few eventful train trips to come at various grounds around the country.

There were, however, to be a couple more notable minibus trips before it all seemed to end. The first one was 30 October 1991, and was a Rumbelows League Cup third round tie at Nottingham Forest. It was an evening game so many of us had time off work or, in my case, off college. The journey up was pretty uneventful. It seemed that the days of binge drinking were slowly declining, and nobody was now turning up wearing slippers after telling his missus that he was just popping out to the shops for the morning paper and pint of milk. I don't know how many we took up that evening, but it was a decent number for an away trip in the middle of the week.

As we approached Nottingham we passed the team coach and gave them a decent round of applause and rendition of 'Goodnight Irene'. I remember Dennis Rofe giving us a wave back, as he was sitting in the front seat of the coach. Nottingham Forest were still in the top flight and were managed by the famous Brian Clough. It was almost as much of an event to say we had seen him in the flesh as it was to play Forest as he was Mr Nottingham Forest back then, and maybe always will be.

We arrived at around 5 p.m., maybe earlier, and parked on a side street near the ground and all walked back to a large pub we had driven past by the River Trent. By all accounts this pub was usually a home team pub, but Rovers were there in numbers and the place was packed out early. It was a great little boozer, to be fair. It was in a great location near the ground, and the river ran alongside. There were even a couple of chefs outside with a gas-fired barbecue on the go and serving food. We had a few pints, and the usual 'Goodnight Irene' song filled the venue. There was a great atmosphere. A few Forest fans came down to join us, but there was never any sign of trouble.

The game itself didn't go our way. We were outplayed by a far better side and went down 2–0.

After the game we got back to the minibus and it seemed that there was no one else around the side street. It was pretty much deserted.

We were all just about to get back in the minibus when a mob of around fifty Nottingham Forest fans came around the corner after having spotted us, and decided to follow us back to where we were parked. We weren't aware of them until that moment and, being massively outnumbered, thought the best bet would be to get the minibus started and make a swift exit.

That was easier said than done. The minibus wasn't going anywhere, as it refused to start. You can imagine the scene: the minibus refused to turn over just like out of some kind of American horror movie as the local loony axe murderer approached its victims, who were seemingly unable to escape. We quickly looked around the bus and grabbed whatever we could use in what seemed like an imminent attack. We grabbed the jack handle, the wheel brace, and the odd bottle left over from earlier. The Forest mob were almost on top of us just as the cavalry arrived in the form of the local mounted police force as they came chasing after the Forest fans. Thankfully at that same time the minibus suddenly sprang into life and we were able to avert what could have been a close shave. Who knows how that one could have turned out.

The next big away day for us came just a few months later as we headed to Anfield, the home of Liverpool Football Club, in an FA Cup fourth round replay on 11 February 1992. This time we all sat in the back of Tony's works transit van. Not the most comfortable way to travel, but who cares? We were on our way to Liverpool to watch Bristol Rovers perform at one of football's most famous stadiums against one of the world's biggest and most famous football clubs. They say Liverpool have a fair reputation of not tolerating away supporters on their patch, and I've read a few books about their mob over the years. But, to be fair, there wasn't any hint of trouble that night as far as I knew. Apart from a few funny looks we got in a couple of pubs near the stadium I pretty much think they accepted us.

The FA Cup tie that night was a great occasion, and Bristol Rovers sold their full allocation of tickets that Liverpool allowed us. I was sitting on the side that is now known as their Centenary Stand so I had a great view of the Anfield Road end, which was sold out and packed with blue and white. The atmosphere was brilliant that night, with both sets of supporters in full voice and over 30,000 fans in attendance. Liverpool's rendition of 'You'll Never Walk Alone' was something else, as was the response by Rovers of 'Goodnight Irene'. I believe both sets of supporters had a mutual respect for each other that night.

The game finished in a 2–1 victory for the hosts, Liverpool, but not before Carl Saunders (our very own Billy Ocean) had given Rovers the lead before half-time with a wonderful strike in front of the Kop. Liverpool brought on a young twenty-year-old Steve McManaman, who was to change the course of the game as he took Rovers apart in the second half. The trip back consisted of talk of what a great display Rovers had put up, along with the talent that the kid McManaman had shown.

Bristol Rovers were relegated the following season (1992/93), and John Ward was now at the helm to rebuild the side. Our next success to note was under John Ward, as we reached the play-offs during the 1994/95 season before losing out at Wembley Stadium 2–1 in the final against Huddersfield Town. The feeling of that defeat outweighed the Wembley trip that day, as I thought we were the better side during the ninety minutes. Going to Wembley that day wasn't about the trip, like it had been in the Leyland Daf Cup. This time it was all about the result. The match could have taken place up on Bristol Downs that afternoon, for all we cared. Promotion was the aim, and unfortunately we came up short. How Marcus Browning hit the bar (his shot would have put us 2–1 up if it had gone in) still haunts me today.

Chapter Ten

Back in Bristol

Bristol Rovers came back to Bristol after a ten-year exile in Bath in August 1996. The first home game of the 1996/97 campaign was played at Twerton Park against Peterborough United, which we won 1–0 in front of just over 6,000 supporters. I'm not sure why, but that day I watched the game from the open terracing in what was called the Bristol End. It seemed strange leaving Twerton Park that afternoon for the final time but the club and its supporters needed to be back in Bristol for its long-term identity, if for nothing else.

Bristol Rovers were returning to play at Bristol Rugby Club's home, the Memorial Ground in Horfield, which was just a stone's throw up the Muller Road from our old Eastville Stadium. Bristol Rugby Club was in deep financial trouble at the time, and offered Rovers the opportunity to purchase part of the stadium to help clear some of their debts. Bristol Rovers eventually completed the full purchase of the ground in 1998, while Bristol Rugby Club continued to struggle financially.

Just for the record, I stood on the then uncovered North Terrace during the first game at the Memorial Ground and watched Rovers draw 1–1 against Stockport County in front of an attendance of 6,380. It is in fact the area of the ground where I have stood ever since, apart from the odd sortie around the stadium just to have the occasional change.

Ian Holloway took over as manager in 1996 and stayed in charge during an exciting few years at Bristol Rovers until he left in early 2001. I enjoyed the time that Ian Holloway was manager. It was a time of some great, entertaining football and near misses in terms of promotion, and we had some great results. In my opinion the club went downhill rapidly after he left and didn't really recover fully, apart from a short spell under Paul Trollope in 2007 until now.

Over the first twenty years since their return back to Bristol in 1996 it has been a typical Bristol Rovers roller coaster ride.

- Play-offs defeat
- Play-offs victory in the final
- Trip to Cardiff's Millennium Stadium in the Johnstone's Paint Trophy Final
- Relegation to non-league football
- Promotion to Division Two after a Conference Final victory at Wembley and promotion again just twelve months later up to Division One.

And who knows what the future has in store for the next few years?

As I've mentioned, we were now more or less past the days of minibus travel. It was now mainly on the train or in our own cars. Jeff had a spell where he was keen to drive anywhere and we both visited a few far-flung venues, like Boston United, Cambridge United, Rushden & Diamonds, Kidderminster Harriers, and Mansfield Town, to name a few. Jeff even went to Kidderminster Harriers on his own once over a Christmas period: that was how keen he was for a while. Now I haven't seen him at a Rovers game for years. I wouldn't be far wrong in saying that the last time he came to a game with us would have been the 2007 Wembley play-off victory over Shrewsbury Town.

Under Ian Holloway we had a few moments to savour, and the big 6–0 hammering of Reading in their own backyard at the Madejski Stadium during February 1999 was one that lives long in the memory. All the goals came in front of the Rovers supporters during the second half as Jamie Cureton and Jason Roberts put in a masterclass showing,

It was during the same season that the four of us – me, Jeff, Allan, and Kev – took an early morning train out of Temple Meads station along with a number of other Bristol Rovers supporters to Barnsley for an FA Cup fifth round tie. The result didn't go well, as we lost to the then Premiership side 5–0. The most memorable part of the day was getting a free and tasty breakfast in a cafe when we stopped off in

Sheffield on our way up. I think we arrived at the cafe at the right time, as the two women serving couldn't keep up with what they were dishing out and who was actually paying. I blame Jeff to this day, as I'm sure he said it was his treat. Whoever treated me ... it was good of them. You can't beat a free fry-up.

Barnsley as a town was pretty grim, to be fair, and it was no surprise that we had to face a bombardment of missiles at the train station after the game. Bottles, bricks, and chunks of wood all came flying our way. God knows what they would have been like if we had won.

The following season (1999/2000) we somehow threw promotion away, if not the title, over the final ten games. Something must have been going on behind the scenes for that to happen, as we went from pole position and promotion certainties to missing out on the play-offs altogether after a last-day defeat at Cardiff City.

The following 2000/2001 season saw us relegated from Division Two into the bottom tier for the first time in the club's history. It was a strange season, and we should never have been in such a situation, but they do say that the table doesn't lie.

Personally I think the upheaval behind the scenes played a huge part in our downfall that year. If it hadn't been for Halifax Town, and only one team down from the bottom tier the following season, we could well have ended up out of the Football League altogether after finishing in twenty-third position (just one off the bottom of the league).

The 2000s, to be honest, weren't much to write home about for Bristol Rovers and our time as supporters, apart from the second half of the 2006/2007 season. Rovers put together a brilliant run after Christmas under the leadership of manager Paul Trollope, reaching the Johnstone Paint Trophy Final. We knocked out Bristol City on the way over a two-leg Southern Area final, and won promotion after a play-off final in the new Wembley Stadium.

At one stage during March we still had one eye on the bottom half of the league table before a strong run of results put us in with a chance of grabbing a final play-off spot if we could win at an already promoted Hartlepool United on the final day. Hartlepool United away was not an easy task, as they were flying and going for the league title. If Hartlepool United had won that afternoon then they would have been crowned divisional champions.

I drove up to to Hartlepool with Kev and Allan and we witnessed a late winner from Rickie Lambert to snatch our play-off spot from Stockport County, who also won their game away at Darlington. The play-offs went perfectly, as we disposed of Linclon City home and away before defeating Shrewsbury Town 3–1 in the final.

What a great day at Wembley we had. The stadium was still only a few games old, and the whole place looked unbelievable. The atmosphere that day was one of the best I've experienced as a Rovers supporter. The moment Sammy Igoe ran the full length of the Wembley turf being chased by a couple of Shrewsbury Town defenders will stay with me forever. It was as if time stood still and everything was happening in slow motion. Once the ball hit the back of the net the scenes of celebrations were amazing among the thousands of Rovers supporters. It was quoted that we had anything between 38,000 to 40,000 there that day.

Coming after the trip to Cardiff's Millennium Stadium, 2007 turned out to be a year to remember. The following three seasons of consolidation back in the renamed Division One were abruptly ended after the 2010/11 season, when we found ourselves back in the basement and in Division Two again.

The encounters with the so-called larger clubs during those seasons back in Division One were a welcome relief. Norwich City, Southampton, Leeds United, and Sheffield Wednesday as league fixtures felt a lot better than Boston United, that's for sure. And a trip down to Southampton midweek when Andy Williams hit a last-minute winner in a 3–2 victory was my personal highlight back in Division One.

Unfortunately relegation came again 2011. We just seemed to drift so quickly, as the football club was reaching its lowest ebb. When we were promoted in 2007 nobody had envisaged ever dropping back into the bottom tier so soon. Watching Bristol Rovers had stopped becoming enjoyable, and a lot of us were slowly drifting away from regularly attending games. Trips away were all but becoming a far and distant memory, as rarely did any of us suggest an away day. It was hard enough to turn up for home games.

Eventually that fateful day in May 2014 was upon us, and it hit us smack bang in the face. We may look back at this as a time when Bristol Rovers received a kick up the backside, one that finally woke the club back up. It had been drifting far too long and had an attitude of, *We are probably too big and too well-supported to drop out of the Football League.* Well, it did happen, and thankfully we responded to it in the right way.

So what now? Well the promotion back to the Football League at the first attempt in 2015 has given everyone a whole new outlook, and watching Bristol Rovers has become much more enjoyable again. And what does the future hold? Well, who knows? Watch this space, as they say.

We currently have a bright new young manager Darrell Clarke in charge: one who could make a name for himself over the coming years, I am sure. Hopefully he stays with us and the football club moves forward with him at the helm. It's great news that he has recently turned down the opportunity to manage a club like Leeds United to stay with us and sign a new three year contract. Maybe now with our new owner Mr Wael Al Qadi coming on board at the start of 2016 he will move the club that we love in the direction we all want it to be heading.

Things have started to look up again for us supporters with two back to back promotions from the Football Conference up to League Division One, and hopefully Division One football will be replaced by Championship football sooner rather than later – which, as Bristol Rovers supporters, we all believe we deserve. Nobody really saw the last two seasons coming, its more Roy of the Rovers than Bristol Rovers.

The future's bright. The future is blue and white.

Chapter Eleven

A Time to Right the Wrongs

The 2013/14 season ended in disaster for everyone who held Bristol Rovers dear to their heart. The club had somehow failed to take on board the real possibilities that we could actually go down from the Football League to a status as a non-league club. The players and management had not done enough to prevent the crisis because I believe they never really thought we could go down. The attitude was this: *Bristol Rovers are far too big and well-supported to face such a prospect.*

However, come the final whistle on the last game of the season at home to Mansfield Town the unthinkable did happen, and Rovers were relegated from Football League Division Two to the depths of despair: the Football Conference; the non-league.

The slide started as late as March with talk on the terraces at the time that Rovers were still in with an outside chance of making a late dash towards the League Two play-offs but, for reasons only the players and management staff can honestly explain, Rovers capitulated into a last-day dogfight which, ultimately, they lost.

Mansfield Town sat in the middle of the table that final afternoon in May at the Memorial Stadium with nothing to play for, and in front of a sell-out attendance of over 10,000 Rovers supporters baying for their blood. It was to be one of those afternoons when everything that could have gone against us did go against us.

I remember having a couple of prematch beers before the game, not really contemplating that we would be returning back home later that afternoon without having got the job done and our league status secured. The week before Kev and I had travelled up to Adams Park, the home of Wycombe Wanderers, along with another large travelling away support and watched us pull off a well-deserved 2–1 victory, which all but sealed our Football League status and should have condemned Wycombe Wanderers back to non-league obscurity.

The Rovers fans joyfully celebrated the scoreline as if the job had been done there and then, and to be honest with you I don't think many people would have argued against it. Going into the final game of the season it was to be any one team from Wycombe Wanderers, Northampton Town, and us who would be joining an already relegated Torquay United. All the pressure was now on a Wycombe Wanderers side that couldn't do anything but win and hope others slipped up as their fate was out of their hands.

Seven days on from what surely would have been a demoralising defeat to Rovers it was to be the Wycombe fans celebrating along with Northampton Town as both sides pulled off victories, which condemned Bristol Rovers on goal different to relegation. Amazingly, it was to be the only time we had actually been in the bottom two places all season. While watching Wycombe the previous week I would never have thought they would pick up a point at Torquay United, let alone win the match 3–0. Northampton Town were basically in the same boat as us with a home clash against Oxford United, and after an early wobble they also ran out comfortable winners once Oxford had been reduced to ten men.

So Bristol Rovers, the oldest football club in Bristol, had lost their proud Football League status. It had been snatched away, and it was an awful gut-wrenching feeling. This wasn't just some relegation. This was more than that. This felt as if the heart of your football club had been publicly ripped out. It wasn't nice, and it was extremely difficult to comprehend. In my opinion too many of the players let the club, themselves, and the supporters down, and you could visualise some of them rushing for the exit doors once the crocodile tears had dried up.

The whole club was at its lowest ebb and, most of all the supporters were. Some fans took out their frustrations immediately after the final whistle by invading the pitch and confronting the visiting supporters from Mansfield Town, while others chose to vent their frustrations at the current board members and at Nick Higgs in particular. I can see how people need someone to blame, as I myself had my own feelings about whose fault it was.

97

The board could have done more – I'm sure they won't deny that – but also, at the end of the day, it's their money and their neck on the line when push comes to shove. Some of their decisions were the right ones and some weren't.

Did they invest enough money into the playing budget at vital stages? Did the various managers given the job over the preceding years care enough for the club? And were the players brought in the right ones?

There are many questions and answers and a mass of opinions among the supporters about what went wrong, but it was a time, however difficult, to stand together and unite as one to get the club back at the earliest opportunity. And that was basically at the first time of asking, however difficult it may or may not be. The club was going to need a lot of fresh blood, and the job ahead was going to be difficult for the players who were going to be asked to come in and do the job.

The new players and staff would need to be mentally strong as well as good enough to wear the famous blue and white quarters, as Bristol Rovers was a wounded animal and things could get very unpleasant very quickly because of it. Players coming in couldn't just come along for the status of playing for a well-supported club and pick up their wages without achieving the goal of immediate promotion.

The arrogance comes from the fact that because of the size and the potential of Bristol Rovers we feel that league football is our right and even League Two football can feel beneath many of the supporters, especially those of us who first started watching Rovers as a second-tier football club playing the likes of Chelsea, West Ham, and Newcastle United, to name a few. A spell at non-league level wasn't going to be a picnic, and football as a whole wasn't going to give us any sympathy whatsoever. Any achievements were going to have to be earned.

Fifteen players were either released or transferred out of the club over the summer period as Rovers and football club manager Darrell Clarke slowly rebuilt a squad capable of making a challenge on the Conference title. Clarke brought in a number of players he had known, trusted, or worked with personally, and who he felt could withstand the pressures of playing for Bristol Rovers in front of a large and demanding crowd week in and week out.

The season was to start with a home game against another former league club, Grimsby Town, who were stuck in the whirlpool of the Conference, having fallen through the trapdoor some seasons earlier. The rest of the non-league welcomed us with open arms as they had another big home and away day to tick off their ground-hopping list and smaller club chairmen were rubbing their hands together in glee, waiting for a decent pay day when the boys from the city came to visit.

The banter pages and forums were quick to warn us how we would be stuck among them for many years to come, and we should get used to it. We were not looking to stay and, thankfully, we didn't. I had bought another season ticket for the 2014/15 season on the back of our penultimate game victory at Wycombe Wanderers, and to say I was looking forward to the season ahead was a million miles from the truth.

It was a long, hard summer in which we had to cope with the Brazilian World Cup tournament splashed all over our television screens, which just seemed to rub salt into our already deep wounds. I had little time for football, and I was glad to see the back of that World Cup.

The game against Grimsby Town had been moved to an earlier kick-off time for live television coverage on BT Sport, further proving that we were now the big fish in the Conference and its members were looking forward to having us in their ranks. I wasn't looking forward to the start of another football season, and to be honest with you I can't ever remember feeling like I did on day one of a new football season.

I had even arranged a driving experience day on the same weekend at Castle Combe race circuit and was looking forward to attending that much more than any football match. If it wasn't for the change of kick-off time I would have gladly missed the football that day, season ticket or no season ticket. I took up my position on the terraces come kick-off and greeted a new-looking Bristol Rovers team, along with a decent crowd of over 7,000.

Grimsby Town was the bookies' favourite, and the feeling was that if there was going to be a difficult game then this was probably the one team we will need to watch. Bristol Rovers edged the match and could

99

have won it, although having said that Grimsby Town did have a glorious chance to snatch it themselves. But, overall, if Grimsby were the biggest threat that we were going to encounter in the Conference then I was reasonably confident that we were going to be there or thereabouts come the end of the season.

The season was up and running, and we had our first point on the board after a steady 0–0 draw to start the season. The Castle Combe driving experience was great as well, so maybe things were going to be all right after all. If things were going to be all right then the next few weeks was the wake-up call, as Rovers were beaten by a physical Barnet side and again at part-time Altrincham, both on the road in the first week. The ship was taking a few early hits and it was not going down too well with the Bristol Rovers supporters, but was bringing great joy to numerous others.

The following weekend I picked up Kev and met up with Allan for a couple of prematch beers, and we discussed what had gone on over the previous couple of games. There were calls for Darrell Clarke's head already, and Kev was warning of a long, hard season to come – which, to be fair, I was thinking to myself as well. I'm sure both of us were planning what we could be doing on Saturday afternoons in the future if things weren't going to change.

'Stick with it,' I said. 'We will be all right. You wait and see,' but at that stage it was more in hope that belief. AFC Telford was the opposition that afternoon and a nervy performance (albeit a 1–0 victory against a side that didn't have much to offer) wasn't really what we needed to settle us down. A win's a win, so they say, and the goal that won it for us was worthy of winning any game, as Ollie Clarke found the back of the Telford net with a great strike early in the second half from outside the penalty area.

Bank holiday Monday was next up, and a local trip to Forest Green Rovers (Oh, how the mighty had fallen). I didn't go and Kev was on holiday, but Allan did. He drove the short distance to watch us come away with another point in what looked like a promising display, and a game that you would say Bristol Rovers were very unlucky not to win. I watched the game in the pub on Ashley Down Road with my brother Glen, nephew Wayne, and few other lads who all happened to be

Rovers supporters. We had all intended on spending the day watching England play India in the one-day international at the Bristol County Ground in Nevil Road but Mother Nature had a big part to play in that one, as we had continuous heavy rain and play didn't even get under way. At least we were able to watch the football in the comfort of a dry pub as a consolation before making our way home via a few of the Gloucester Road hostelries.

Halifax Town were next up at the Memorial Stadium, and it was a late Rovers winner against a decent-looking Halifax team that saw us pick up another three points, as we won 2–1. We weren't setting the league alight but the team looked as if it was giving its all … and we were picking up useful points, as we kept within touching distance of the play-off places and early leaders.

Another wake-up call was just around the corner as Rovers again came unstuck to another part-time outfit when they visited Braintree Town. Rovers suffered an embarrassing 2–0 reverse and saw a small outbreak of crowd trouble, as some supporters understandably found it all too much to bear. Darrell Clarke was again under pressure as a small number of fans called for his head, and he later went on record saying he felt his job could be on the line. I can recall him saying in a radio interview a week or so after the Braintree result after Rovers had just won,

'Well, that should keep my job for another week.'

The Braintree Town embarrassment seemed to be the match that kick-started a run of five victories on the bounce, and had Kev, Allan, and me deciding to make the evening trip after work down to Eastleigh FC.

Eastleigh is basically Southampton, and it was hard to imagine that only a few years earlier we had been heading to St Mary's, the home of Southampton FC in League One. We returned to Bristol that night after playing Southampton with all three points after winning 3–2 in dramatic fashion, when Andy Williams hit an unstoppable shot that burst the net in front of the Rovers supporters. The scenes after the game and the drive home were pretty special, to say the least.

Southampton was now just a distant memory as Bristol Rovers and its supporters headed to the south coast once more. Rovers took over a

101

thousand supporters to Eastleigh's tiny Silverlake Stadium and it was pleasing to see we had sold out of our allocation of tickets in a short space of time.

I had to ask myself as I stood looking around the stadium what had happened to us. It was less than twelve months ago that we were filling out the away end at Birmingham City in the FA Cup. I know that no team has a divine right to play league football, but this really was hard to stomach. Why did it have to happen to us? There was no time to feel sorry for ourselves. If we were to get back at the first attempt then we needed to knuckle down and come to places like this, work bloody hard, and make sure we came away with a result. The match finished up as a 1–1 draw, and it turned out to be a decent point at the end of the night.

Eastleigh have been recently on the crest of a wave, and have had a lot of money injected into them from a wealthy businessman who was determined to bring league football to the town. They had invested heavily in the playing side and had a fair amount of experienced ex-league players in their ranks, who must have been picking up a tidy wage to be tempted to go there in the first place.

Rovers fell behind, and also had Steve Mildenhall sent off all during the first half-hour of the game, and we were up against some dubious referee decisions, to say the least. Ollie Clarke struck the equaliser with another long-range unstoppable strike in the second half, and from that point onward it looked as if there was only going to be one winner.

There was to be another twist in the tale as Rovers lost another player when goalscorer Ollie Clarke was shown the red card and sent off near the end of the game, and Rovers were forced to play out the final minutes with only nine players on the pitch. I went away from the match thinking that the new crop of players were beginning to show an awful lot of fight for the shirt, and were sticking together as a team under the guidance of Darrell Clarke. It was a result that gave me hope once again that maybe this team would be celebrating come May.

The journey to and from the south coast from Bristol isn't the easiest journey, but at least we were in reasonably good spirits. Bristol Rovers went on to pick up five more points from their next three games, consisting of draws against Dover Athletic Aldershot Town and a 1–0 win against Dartford. I had somehow missed ever visiting Aldershot during our and their Football League days, so the three of us – Kev, me, and Allan, decided to make the trip up the M4.

We drove up with Kev at the wheel and me in the usual co-pilot seat, to ensure that we take the right motorway junctions and roundabout exits. It's a pretty responsible job as there was many a time when we came off too early or too late and ended up driving miles out of our way, missing out on valuable drinking time. We have had a few laughs getting lost over the years, it all added to the fun of the day.

There was a time when I went to Cambridge United a few years previously with Jeff Wherlock and another guy called Darren. On the way back from the game we found ourselves heading north towards Peterborough. By the time the mistake was rectified and we turned around this had added at least an extra hour to our journey. It was also the day Darren nearly froze to death as I insisted that I had the front window down a little, as I was suffering from a thumping headache from a few too many lagers the night before at skittles. I'll stand by the same comment I made that day. If Jeff had only switched the heating down slightly in the car then I wouldn't have needed the window open so much. Jeff was always one to make full use of the climate control in his car, and that usually meant he had the heaters on at full blast.

The Aldershot trip was one of those days that Bristol Rovers supporters all seemed to have the same idea about having an away day, and the team was backed by another large travelling support. This had not gone unnoticed and had been written about in the national press, and was being mentioned widely on social media the following Monday morning. The atmosphere that afternoon was one of the best I had heard for quite a while at an away match. The large Bristol Rovers following were mainly housed under cover, and therefore, as I have mentioned before, the sound always tends to be that much more impressive. The Aldershot Town supporters played their part, especially as they had a drummer, who never seemed to let up all afternoon. I'm not a fan of drummers at football matches but, to be fair, it did add to the game's atmosphere that afternoon.

If you have ever been to Aldershot Town's football stadium you

103

will know it's not one to write home about, and the toilet facilities reminded me of a throwback to something from the 1980s. I think I missed a good ten to fifteen minutes while queuing for use of a single portable trailer loo, and it wasn't going down to well with everyone. A few harsh words were being directed at the stewards on duty. It wasn't their fault, but it was them who took the stick.

The match itself was a pretty entertaining affair, which finished up as a 2–2 draw. Rovers allowed the game to slip, if I'm honest, but as in every game now we were deemed as the big boys of the league and it seemed that many teams and its supporters were raising their game against us. However, it was another point on the road and kept us on a good run.

Forest Green Rovers was the next fixture, and it was to be one of only two more defeats during the remainder of the season that we were to suffer. Forest Green came with a well-executed plan and bullied us from start to finish, drawing on every trick in the book to spoil the flow of the game. I think Bristol Rovers probably learnt a lot that afternoon, which stood them in good stead for the remainder of the season and eventually for our play-off semi-final clashes with them.

A win and three more draws were registered before Bristol Rovers took on the leaders, Barnet, at the Memorial Stadium at the end of November. The 2–1 victory didn't really reflect the dominant display Rovers put in that night. However, the three points gave us all the belief that we were going to be giving it a real go and sent a reminder to Barnet FC and the rest of the promotion contenders that Bristol Rovers were not going to be messing around and stewing in the Conference for longer than necessary.

The remaining matches before Christmas saw Rovers pick up a decent points return, and we went into the new year with a couple of wins and a couple of draws. If there was one problem to address it was the need to turn a few more of the draws into wins, as there was only the one place on offer for outright promotion. Otherwise we would have the lottery of the play-off to contest at the end of the season, which was made up of the teams finishing from positions two to five.

A hard-fought win over Gateshead at the Memorial Stadium just as we all broke up for Christmas saw Rovers win in a tense but entertaining game on a Friday night that was played out in front of live television coverage. Bristol Rovers twice came from a goal down to run out 3–2 winners and gain a vital three points. The terraces were bouncing that night as we again had to overcome a team that were treating the match with Bristol Rovers as their own cup final, with the added spice of knowing they were also performing in front of live television cameras.

As we drove home from the game we knew that if we didn't achieve promotion it wouldn't be because of a lack of trying, as you could clearly see that the players were giving it their all. They were giving us pride back in the shirt, which had been evidently missing in recent seasons.

Boxing Day saw us bring home all three points after a win at Torquay United, a trip that we had usually driven to in recent seasons, but with Christmas and families to think about it was decided to give this one a miss.

We were all back on the terraces a few days later with a home clash against Macclesfield Town, a side that were also within a shout of automatic promotion, or the play-offs at least. After a hard first half Bristol Rovers finally wore down a dogged Town side and ran out comfortable 4–0 winners. The North Enclosure celebrated the one-sided second half by waving an array of mobile phone torchlights around in the air, which rubbed off around the stadium and, I must admit, looked a pretty good sight. The good run of results continued into the new year. Rovers were slowly bringing Barnet back into range as the title race gathered speed.

The first week of January saw Darrell Clarke named as Manager of the Month for December. It was the second time he had been awarded that honour during the season. Further intent was shown by Rovers when Jermaine Easter was signed in the transfer window from League One side Millwall. The former Welsh international was another warning sign to the rest of the Conference that Bristol Rovers were not looking to hang around for longer than necessary, and that signing was also backed up with Adam Dawson (on loan from Leicester City) who proved to be a handful for the rest of the Conference defences he took

105

on during the remainder of the campaign.

Grimsby Town were continuing to be both Bristol Rovers and Barnet's nearest contenders, but they never once got close enough to put any real pressure on the top two. The volume of support at both home and away games was also gathering pace, and it was further emphasised that Rovers were far too big a football club to be playing at Conference level at Woking FC.

The trip to Woking during the middle of January saw hundreds of travelling Rovers supporters left locked outside of the ground, as Woking couldn't cope with the sheer numbers of Gasheads turning up in their thousands. The game finished in a 0–0 draw as Woking, like every other team we encountered throughout the season, seemed to raise their game on the day by putting everything on the line to make things as difficult as possible. If Rovers were going to win promotion it wasn't going to be given to us without a fight.

The following couple of months looked set to be a defining point in the season as we had to travel to a few of the sides who were all fighting over the top half-dozen or so positions in the League, and to make matters slightly more difficult the majority of them were as far north as they come.

First up in February was a home clash with former Football League foes Lincoln City. Lincoln were the side that Rovers had disposed of in the successful 2007 League Two promotion campaign, and it seemed strange that we were meeting them for the first time at home since that time. There's no sentiment in sport and Lincoln had now fallen on hard times, like a few ex-Football League sides. Lincoln City, as I remember, was always a tough Football League fixture over the number of years I've been following Bristol Rovers. However, that afternoon Lincoln City were well beaten on the day 2–0, and the Rovers momentum continued.

Next up was a long trek to promotion rival Grimsby Town at Blundell Park. Rovers came away with a well-deserved 1–0 victory in a performance which sent out another message to all our promotion rivals that we were in it till the end. Bristol Rovers Football Club were not going away. Promotion was our only goal, and hopefully nothing was going to stop us achieving it.

Two nervy home wins followed against Altrincham and Braintree Town, 1–0 and 2–1 respectively. In both games the opposition put their bodies on the line again as we fought to break them down. Throughout all these games the Rovers crowds continued to get fully behind the team, which I'm sure helped the team over the line and at times helped intimidate our smaller opposition.

The final match of February was the trip to Gateshead. Gateshead had looked a decent side when we played them just before Christmas, and were one of the sides in the hunt for a possible play-off place. A decent following of Gasheads made the trip via train, plane, coach, and car, and were rewarded with a victory and a wonder goal from Ellis Harrison. Darrell Clarke had finished the month with five wins from five difficult- looking games, and was to receive his third Manager of the Month award.

Barnet's huge lead at the top of the Conference League table was now down to a couple of points, and going into the last nine games it was looking like a two-horse race to the end of the season. Grimsby Town, who were in third position, were just about hanging on to the coat-tails of both Barnet and Rovers, hoping for a slip-up.

I was enjoying the season much more than I had ever envisaged. Matches were being won, and the atmosphere was pretty good on the terraces. I woke up on a Saturday looking forward to attending a Bristol Rovers game again, a feeling that had been missing over the previous couple of seasons. I know it was only the Conference but, after an awful start to the season, things were looking rosy and promotion looked to be odds-on, well that's what I thought, as I am ever the optimist even in times of adversity.

After a decent February and a few prematch beers at the Civil Service Club on Filton Avenue next up to the slaughter was Eastleigh, a side with a millionaire chairman and plenty of money to chuck around on players who could boost wearing the 'Been there, done that' ex-Football League T-shirts. Whether they were journeymen looking for a decent pay day in non-league football or players with a bit of fight still left in them to achieve something else in their careers I was not sure, but they proved to be a very difficult nut to crack that first

Saturday afternoon in March. To be honest, they came with a game plan to slow the game down and frustrate Rovers at every opportunity, and you have to hand it to them. Their tactics that afternoon worked a treat.

I didn't find them a good side to watch, but when you're up against teams like that then you have to learn to break them down and be prepared to chance your style of play as the game develops. Unfortunately that afternoon we didn't adapt quickly enough and found ourselves on the wrong side of a 2–1 home defeat. It was a setback, and a similar type of defeat to the one we had we suffered against Forest Green Rovers at home earlier in the campaign. The worrying thing was that we may have to come across either Eastleigh or FGR again later in the end of season play-offs and so far it seemed that their style of play was the one that had given us our only real trouble to date. We had to ensure that the lessons learnt from these encounters were taken on board, and they were not going to come back and upset us again.

After a poor start in the North of England away at Halifax Town, Rovers fought back to come home with a point and a 2–2 draw, and then a comfortable home win over Aldershot Town on the following Friday night put us in pole position overnight. Hopefully that would add to the pressure on the chasing pack when they all kicked off on the Saturday afternoon.

The following weekend BT Sport had again chosen a Bristol Rovers clash for live Saturday lunchtime television, and this one was at Macclesfield Town. Macclesfield isn't on our doorstep, so the chances of travelling up to Moss Road when it was being broadcast in the comfort of my living room was never a really a contest.

The match was a poor 0–0 draw played on an awful pitch on a wet and windy day, and to be fair it wasn't a great advert for football. It would have been Rovers if anyone was going to win it, as they looked the more dangerous. In terms of league positions it wasn't a bad point, but with Barnet still picking up points it felt like two points dropped.

Five games remained, and I thought that if we could win all five then the title would be ours, as Barnet still had a couple of awkward-looking fixtures to negotiate. Grimsby were still in with an outside shout but they would have needed both Rovers and Barnet to fall away badly and, to be fair, neither of us ever really looked like being drawn back into the chasing pack.

April had begun, and first up in the Easter fixtures was Chester City at home. Rovers stormed to an easy 5–1 win, and set off for an Easter Monday away trip in the Midlands against Kidderminster Harriers. Another huge away following watched Rovers grind out a 3–0 victory. Barnet and Rovers were now battling it out neck and neck at the top of the league, both sides swapping places as matches swayed to and fro during the ninety minutes.

Three matches remained. The result of the next one was Bristol Rovers 2, Southport 0. Then two matches remained. Barnet were at Kidderminster Harriers, and Rovers were away to Dover Athletic.

Barnet had gone behind at Kidderminster before coming back to pick up a valuable point. All Rovers needed was the win at Dover and the title could be secured the following weekend with a victory over struggling Alfreton Town. The pressure was on, and as Rovers approached the final couple of minutes of the game they had a 2–1 lead and held the top spot in the live league table. But in true Bristol Rovers fashion, which we had all become accustomed to as supporters of the club, Dover Athletic snatched a late equaliser. The match finished 2–2, and Barnet had retained their one-point average at the top of the league table.

The final weekend of the regular season saw both Barnet and Bristol Rovers finishing off with home fixtures. I was longing for the weekend to come around as quickly as possible so that we could get to the Memorial Stadium and hopefully cheer Bristol Rovers on to the win that they needed to ensure that we were going to push Barnet all the way to the final kick of the season. I was hoping that the pressure would get to Barnet, and they would somehow throw it away by either losing or drawing their last final game.

Our final fixture was against Alfreton Town, who were in a dire position and facing relegation if they didn't themselves get something out of the game. It was a typical end of season setting: big crowd, high spirits, and a sunny afternoon. A record attendance of 11,085 for a Conference game was set inside the stadium, beating a previous best achieved by Oxford United some years earlier during their short spell in the football Conference.

Bristol Rovers were welcomed on to the field of play to a tremendous noise, and there was no doubt that the supporters were going to play their part. We just hoped that the players would not freeze or be left with any regrets come the end of the ninety minutes. Rovers took an early lead and for a few minutes once again had led the live table, before Barnet themselves went a goal ahead in their match. It was the only time we were ahead of Barnet that afternoon as they comfortably won their match, and took the title by a point. The Rovers fans were to be treated to a goal fest, as we ran out 7–0 winners over an Alfreton side that couldn't cope with the lively Bristol Rovers side that afternoon, and it condemned Alfreton to relegation to the Conference League North. Bristol Rovers were heading into the play-offs with a match over two legs against Forest Green Rovers, while Eastleigh were up against Grimsby Town. Bristol Rovers went into the matches with a huge amount of confidence, and we needed to put right a draw and a defeat in the league encounters with Forest Green Rovers.

Of the other two sides that made it into the play-offs I personally was hoping that Grimsby Town would come through their tie. I'm sure our players and the majority of our supporters would have preferred to meet Grimsby Town in front of a much larger crowd at Wembley Stadium than the outfit with much smaller support, Eastleigh.

So the play-offs and our route back to the Football League after just one season away were upon us.

It was 29 April 2015: Forest Green Rovers versus Bristol Rovers in the first leg at The New Lawn, the home of the Gloucestershire outfit. If we were to put right the wrongs of our earlier league clashes then this was the time and the place to do it. Bristol Rovers supporters as usual sold out their allocation of tickets within hours of them being release for sale. Forest Green Rovers were not keen on allowing us to have too many, as I'm sure they wanted to keep their home leg as much in their favour as possible. What they had not banked on was that Bristol Rovers are a well-supported football club, and if all else fails when trying to obtain a ticket in a sold-out away end then why not try and purchase tickets for the home section? It wasn't as if Forest Green Rovers were going to be purchasing that many themselves, was it?

Eventually the club officials at Forest Green cottoned on that many of their tickets for sale online were being snapped up by supporters with Bristol postcodes, and they then made a decision to cancel and refund anybody they believe was actually a Bristol Rovers supporter. If they had allowed us a bigger allocation in the first place then I'm sure none of this would have happened, and Forest Green Rovers would have made a few extra quid as well.

Luckily the tie was to be shown live on television, so at least we had the opportunity to watch it that way. It was disappointing to see many empty seats in the Forest Green Rovers section of the ground. Surely it would have made commercial sense to sell these seats to supporters who were desperate to be there and watch the match live. It's OK to watch football from your armchair, but nothing beats or compares with the buzz of being at a match and the passion of a football crowd.

Bristol Rovers started the game like a train, and it was clear they meant business. Matty Taylor gave us the lead during a first half in which we could have and should have had the tie out of sight. Forest Green had a brief spell during the second half, but Bristol Rovers were worthy 1–0 winners in a game that saw Bristol Rovers striker Ellis Harrison being shown a red card during the latter stages of the second half.

The Forest Green Rovers tactics were typical of those we had witnessed earlier in the season. The way they niggled at their opponents was certainly no different from our previous encounters with them, but this time we seemed to be a lot wiser to their style.

The second leg took place on Sunday 3 May in front of a full house at the Memorial Stadium, Bristol. Bristol Rovers once again set about the Forest Green side from the first whistle, scoring a goal in both halves to comfortably run out 2–0 winners on the day and 3–0 winners overall on aggregate. It was a good professional all-round performance, and we were just one game away from returning back to the Football League at the first time of asking.

Darrell Clarke took some of his back-room staff across to the local Victoria public house on the Gloucester Road after the game, and they enjoyed a pint with some of the Bristol Rovers supporters. It was a good way for them to relax for an hour or so before the serious business of getting the team ready for a play-off final at Wembley in a couple of weeks' time.

A great piece of footage was soon doing the rounds on social media of Darrell Clarke singing along with the supporters, which further emphasised the desire he had to ensure that Bristol Rovers were going back to where we knew we belong – and that's the Football League. I was feeling pretty confident, to be honest, that we would be the ones celebrating at the end of the Wembley Stadium final. The final obstacle that lay in wait was to be Grimsby Town.

Grimsby Town overcame Eastleigh pretty comfortably, and they tried to get themselves further up for the clash with a media-run campaign from their local newspaper by having a dig at Darrell Clarke, possibly in the hope that it may unsettle him and the team in their preparations for the match ahead. They were hoping his singalong with the Bristol Rovers supporters at the Vic would work in favour of Grimsby and backfire against us.

In all honesty it did nothing to dent our morale, and probably added to the fact that we had a job to do on the pitch against them. Grimsby's local press said it was disrespectful, and tried to whip up the Grimsby Town support. They didn't mention the way their own club players and supporters danced around the pitch after their Eastleigh victory, which had ensured their own passage into the final. Anyway, it wasn't bothering us. We had bigger fish to fry, and as fish is well known to be associated with Grimsby Town, then they were our fish.

There were two weeks before the final at Wembley, so there was plenty of time for the players from both sides to get themselves ready for the big day. Tickets were soon on sale to supporters and within a day or so of them going on sale I could sleep soundly, knowing that I had mine in the safekeeping of Allan Church. It wasn't long that a coach had been sorted out as well, and our seats were confirmed on the coach arranged by my brother's mate Dave.

Dave Hardcastle was one of the old-school Rovers fans from the good old days back in the Tote End and Eastville Stadium. There's many a story Dave has told us about the good old days of the football and numerous encounters he came across when following Bristol Rovers. Dave's a sound bloke and I have got to know him over the years, due to Glen. I have been to football, cricket, and the Cheltenham Festival on Gold Cup Day, and can honestly say that they are always top days out. Allan, Kev, and his daughter Maddison were making the trip up to Wembley for the game, and had also reserved seats on the coach. Glen and a number of his family came along as well, so our coach was pretty much made up of families heading up for the game and our ultimate promotion.

The build-up usually is a nervous week or so of counting down the hours until the big day arrives, and it was no different this time. For whatever reason I felt confident that the right result and outcome was almost a certainty. I had felt reasonably confident all season that we were going to bounce back at the first attempt, so why change now?

What is a Wembley play-off final without a new T-shirt, scarf, or flag? So in the week leading up to the game I shot across at lunchtime from work and visited the Bristol Rovers club shop at the Memorial Stadium in Horfield and purchased myself a blue and white polo shirt ready for the day. Ticket sales were going pretty well, and we were expecting to take just over the 30,000 mark. It was not quite as many as the 2007 League Two play-off final, but a pretty good turnout nonetheless.

Sunday 17 May 2016 was going to be another pivotal day in the long history of Bristol Rovers Football Club. Could they bounce back into the Football League at the first attempt? It was one year on from the depressing scenes that had greeted us all at the Memorial Stadium after our relegation, and it was an immediate opportunity to put it right.

Bristol woke up to clear blue sunny skies, and as I wandered around the garden drinking an early morning coffee (aptly from a Bristol Rovers mug while gathering my thoughts on the huge day that lay ahead) I just knew it was going to be OK. I looked up to a blue and white sky. It was a sign (well, that's what I told myself).

Kev came over with Allan and Maddison to pick me up just after 8

113

a.m., and we set off to meet up with the others and catch our coach from the Shield and Dagger in Whitchurch. Next stop Wembley Stadium, London.

Once on the road the general chit-chat was about the game ahead. Most were confident of a Rovers win and the importance of it, due to the money implications of another season outside the Football League and how that would impact on the playing budget and the club as a whole. Bristol Rovers were still in a long-drawn-out case over the sale of the Memorial Stadium to the supermarket chain Sainsbury's. The eventual outcome was not only delaying the anticipated move to a new purpose-built stadium in partnership with the University of the West of England (UWE) but was obviously a huge drain on resources in fighting one thing after another, including local residents and traders who had set up their anti-supermarket protest groups.

During a stop-off at the Membury service station, along with what seemed like half of Bristol, I had a beer and a bite to eat and watched the never-ending flow of cars, coaches, and minibuses full of eagerly anticipating Rovers supporters enter and exit the service station, all heading towards London and Wembley Stadium.

The last time I had visited Wembley was back in 2007 for the Bristol Rovers successful League Two play-off victory over Shrewsbury Town (3–1). It was one of the first matches played at the new Wembley Stadium, and the whole stadium had a new smell about it that day. In the eight years since that day a lot of infrastructure had gone up around it, and the outside looked completely different to my last visit. Once parked it was time to enjoy a cider and have a quick look around the outside of the stadium while posing for a picture or two generally soaking up the atmosphere.

One of the new buildings that had gone up since my last visit was the impressive-looking Hilton Hotel. The Hilton Hotel had a large rooftop terrace called the Sky Bar, and a number of us made our way up to the top floor. I didn't think we stood a chance of getting into the Hilton but, to my amazement, we were all allowed in and made our way up to the top-floor Sky Bar. The view from the open terrace at the top was pretty cool, and it was great to have a few beers while watching supporters from both clubs make their way into Wembley.

An hour or so later it was time to make our way into the stadium and find our seats. The atmosphere was building up nicely and, to be fair, the Grimsby Town supporters were making a decent noise as well. Whether or not it would have been as noticeable without the beating of a drum I'm not so sure, but credit where it's due. It certainly added to the overall atmosphere inside the stadium. It's the very reason why playing a side such as Grimsby Town was always going to be far better than the smaller clubs from the Conference would have been. A record Conference play-off final crowd of 47,029 was inside the stadium to witness the afternoon's events unfold.

The two sides were met with a sea of noise as they entered the field of play just before kick-off, and the rendition of 'Goodnight Irene' was enough to have the hairs standing up on the back of your neck. This was it! There was no turning back now as we got set for a nervous couple of hours. There's something about supporting your own team which gives you a feeling like nothing else in sport.

Typically for Bristol Rovers, they conceded a goal within a couple of minutes of the start of the match. Grimsby Town broke down our right and somehow after a few bounces off the heel of Tom Lockyer and the chest of Will Puddy we were one down with barely two minutes on the clock. Thankfully it was still early in the game and I felt confident of us bouncing back. Grimsby Town certainly gave it a good go, and put us under a fair amount of pressure for the first quarter of an hour before we slowly eased our way back into the game. There was a call for Will Puddy, the Bristol Rovers keeper, to be given a red card after he came running out of his area and looked to have handled the ball just outside the box. It could have been a game changer but as we had defenders rushing back the referee decided that adequate punishment would be to issue a yellow card, along with the resulting free kick for Grimsby Town. Thankfully nothing came of the free kick and the score remained at 1–0.

It wasn't long before Rovers were back on level terms, and the relief I felt was massive. The Grimsby Town defence failed to clear a ball in their box on a couple of occasions and the ball fell at the feet of Ellis Harrison, who thundered home the equaliser. The majority of the stadium erupted, and we were back on terms at 1–1. It wasn't long before we had a clear penalty decision go against us, as Matty Taylor rounded their keeper and looked odds-on to put us 2–1 up before he was clipped and brought down in the area. In hindsight the referee may well have looked at levelling out two very close decisions in favour of either side as he waved away the Bristol Rovers players' protests. I have watched the incident on DVD a number of times since and it's clear in my mind that it was a penalty, so I suppose things possibly evened themselves up during the ninety minutes.

It was half-time. The teams went in at 1–1, and for the remainder of the second half both sides cancelled each other out. I had joked on the coach travelling up that the match would be tight and go all the way to a penalty shoot-out. Little did I know at the time, but that was actually what we would be heading for.

Both sides had half chances during the extra time period, but one chance that I have locked in my mind was Chris Lines of Bristol Rovers firing over the bar from a clear position inside the penalty box with no more than a minute or two remaining on the clock, just before the end of the extra time. It wasn't to be, so we would all have to endure a penalty shoot-out and the obvious stresses than would bring.

Darrell Clarke had just enough time during the 120 minutes play to bring off our goalkeeper Will Puddy and replace him with the much larger frame of our substitute goalkeeper Steve Mildenhall. Let's hope this was going to be an inspired substitution, we all thought. One thing with Clarkey: he wasn't ever afraid to change things around.

The penalty shoot-out was to be at the end of the stadium that housed the Grimsby Town supporters, so the advantage was with them. I'm sure when you see a few thousand arms waving around in your line of sight it must be slightly off-putting when you're feeling a little under pressure and about to take an important penalty.

Chris (he's one of our own) Lines for Rovers was the first to step up in the shoot-out. As he walked forward I thought, 'Here goes.' There was no turning back. It was now or never. 'Please, God, let it be us,' I thought.

Linesy hammered home the first spot with a right-footed kick into the bottom right corner. The score was 1–0. Grimsby returned the favour, with Bristol Rovers old boy Craig Disley making it 1–1.

Matty Taylor was up next. He had missed a couple during the season (one was actually at Grimsby earlier in the season). Fingers crossed. Matty made no mistake this time, as the ball hit the bottom right-hand corner of the net. Their keeper had guessed right, but thankfully couldn't get a decent hand to stop it. It was 2–1 to Bristol Rovers.

Grimsby made it 2–2. This was tense.

Next up for Rovers was Lee Brown, who made no mistake. What a penalty he hit. He left-footed it into the top left-hand corner of the net as the Grimsby keeper went the wrong way. It was now 3–2 to Rovers.

Next to step up for Grimsby was Jon-Paul Pittman. The stadium erupted as he sent his kick high over the bar. I think it was closer to hitting the moon than the back of the net. My heart was now unhealthily beating far too fast, as we had gained the advantage.

The next penalty was going to be massive, even more massive than the one before and the one before that. They were all massive, but if we could keep our heads now ... Angelo Balanta walked forward. Come on, my son ... Balanta made it 4–2 as he placed an unstoppable right-footed shot into the bottom left-hand corner of the Grimsby goal. Yesss!

The pressure was on Grimsby. A miss and we were up. The Grimsby Town player under pressure comfortably found the back of the net. It was 4–3 to Rovers.

Again, the next penalty was massive. 'Bristol Rovers could actually do this here and now,' I thought. 'Please, God let us score this one. Please, please, please.' I wasn't sure if I should watch or look the other way.

Lee Mansell walked forward, holding the ball, and placed it carefully on the spot and stepped back. The next few seconds just seemed to be in slow motion as he ran forward and hit the football right-footed into the top right-hand corner of the net. The football hit the back of the net. Rovers had won it 5–3 in the shoot-out.

Bristol Rovers were back at the first time of asking: back into the Football League. The Bristol Rovers players ran across the pitch to celebrate the promotion, along with scorer Lee Mansell. The Bristol Rovers manager Darrell Clarke was sprinting in the opposite direction and heading towards the Rovers supporters, who were now jumping around in sheer joy and sheer relief of the achievement. I was jumping around not really knowing what to do.

On our last winning Wembley trip, against Shrewsbury Town, I had smacked my shins into the plastic seat in front of me before charging down the steps and grabbing anyone who was nearby. This time I managed to again tear the skin from my shins as I hit the plastic seats in front of me while spinning and bouncing around like some mad kangaroo. Bristol Rovers were back and boy, it felt such a relief.

I would have been a liar if I said I could have faced another season in the Conference. Staying at that level was really not an option for us. It would have been a disaster. You have got to feel a little sorry for sides that have dropped into the Conference and then struggle to bounce back. It was not a nice league, but it could now be just the kick up the backside Bristol Rovers needed to ensure that we now start progressing again.

Thank you, Rovers. Thank you, God. And thank you Darrell Clarke, and everyone who got us back were we surely belong. I was ecstatic. It felt as if my head was about to explode. The journey home wasn't one of massive celebration. It was one of smug accomplishment, of getting the job done, and of knowing that the wrongs of May 2014 had been put right.

We reached the bright lights of Bristol at around 10 p.m. that night. The city was a different place again. It had two Football League clubs, and Bristol Rovers were back where they belong. We were back in the Football League.

The 2015/16 season opened up with a home fixture back in League Two against Northampton Town. We lost the match 1-0 but the relief of being back in the football league so soon was massive.

Little did we know that afternoon, that come May 7th at our last home game of the season just nine months later we would be celebrating back-to-back promotions?

What a fairytale! How things can change in such a short period of time.

Following Bristol Rovers Football Club is a rollercoaster ride and it's one that we tend not to want to get off.

From August 2014 to August 2016 we have jumped from the status of a non-league Football Conference team, back up into the Football

League and our place in Division One.
Who knows where Bristol Rovers are going to take us next?.

Chapter Twelve

My All-Time First XI

I thought this would be easy at first, but it wasn't. Picking an all-time starting XI proved to be a lot more difficult than I had originally expected. Bristol Rovers have had some great players over the years that I have been watching them, and if we could have put them all together in one team I'm sure they would have made a tidy Premiership side.

I also thought it would be interesting to also add my all-time manager in the list and, for a bit of fun, his assistant. Again we have had some good managers in this period and some right lemons, who were either out of their depth at our club or just didn't know what Bristol Rovers was all about and just couldn't understand what Rovers means to us Gasheads.

Bristol Rovers are not your ordinary football club. Bristol Rovers are so much more than that. What we have is something that, unless you have blue blood ruining through your veins, you will find very hard to understand. Throughout the time I've followed them it's never been straightforward, and to be honest I don't think it ever will be.

Eastville, Twerton Park, the Memorial Stadium, a small time away at Ashton Gate, two fires, numerous stadium build proposals, planning permission granted, planning permission revoked, high court judges, the Secretary of State, protest groups, the highs and lows of promotion and relegation, and the drop into the Conference and non-league football for a season before bouncing back at the first attempt.

You name it and I'm sure Bristol Rovers has faced it, which has all made following this football club one hell of a roller coaster ride of emotions. It has tested the best of us over the years, and will continue to in many years to come. I'm sure of that.

OK, so let's get back to picking this side. As with any team, it's all down to a matter of opinions, and some players here you may not have chosen yourselves, I'm sure. But, as they say, one man's love is another man's poison, or something like that.

Right. I'm going to start at the back, so first up it's got to be the goalkeeper. Now I've seen a number of keepers over the years, starting in the early days with a young Martin Thomas, Phil Kite, and the evergreen Ray Cashley and Ron Green all spending time between the sticks. These guys were the first keepers who came to mind from the early days of my following Rovers before along came a stream of others, including the very reliable Brian Parkin and a fans' favourite, Nicky Culkin.

All were tidy keepers over the years but there is one who just jumps out as the best one in my opinion, and that's Nigel Martyn. There's a great story behind how he came to the club back in the late eighties, when he was discovered by the Bristol Rovers tea lady while away in Cornwall during the close season.

So the story goes that she told the then manager Gerry Francis to go and have a look at this guy. And to cut a long story short Francis did, and signed him on the spot. The rest of the story is history, as he was to become the first £1 million goalkeeper when he was signed from Bristol Rovers to Crystal Palace a few years later. This guy was brilliant, and from day one you could see he was going to make it big. There you go, the first player on the team sheet. Our Number One: Nigel Martyn.

Picking a back four was difficult. I jotted loads of names down, crossing them out and rewriting them again before I came up with my final selection. In the end I have decided to go with Gary Mabbutt and Andy Tilson as my central defensive partnership.

Gary Mabbutt played back in the old Eastville days, and I can just remember him being a young, no-nonsense defender who had to defend against some big centre forwards back then, and always holding his own.

I suppose it was no surprise he made his name at Tottenham Hotspur, playing well over 450 games for the North London club and captaining the side. He also was to become a full England international. To play alongside him I eventually went with Andy Tillson. I know I probably watched other players during the early

121

eighties and nineteen in this position who may have been more deserving, but I can't honestly recall anyone who was like Andy Tilson.

He took no messing, and in my eyes was as reliable as anyone who I've seen there over the years. He played for Grimsby Town and Queens Park Rangers before arriving at Rovers in 1992.

I had considered Billy Clark, Steve Elliott, and Geoff Twentyman Jr., but Andy Tillson just snatches it for me. And, after all, he has been our record signing for many years now. An amount like £370,000 was a lot of money back in 1992, especially for us.

The left and right back roles was another difficult task but I'm going to ask my players to be adaptable, and I'm going for Michael Smith at left back and Vaughan Jones to play at right back.

I also looked at the no-nonsense Scot Ian Alexander, our current left back Lee Brown, and a young player from the eighties: Neil Slatter. Ian Alexander was a character, and there was many a time I would see him out on the town after a game on a Saturday night in Bristol letting his hair down. Good old Ian.

Lee Brown came to us in 2011, after starting out at Queens Park Rangers. He showed an awful lot of loyalty to Bristol Rovers when he decided to stay with the club after the relegation to the Conference. He could have left after attracting interest from league clubs, but stayed to ensure that the club bounced back at its first attempt. There's not a lot of loyalty in football nowadays, and this has made him a favourite in many supporters' eyes.

It was pleasing to see that he was also rewarded in some way by receiving his international call-up and England caps by representing the England C team, an opportunity he wouldn't have been given if he would have decided to leave.

Neil Slatter was a tall, long-legged young Welsh lad with a bit of pace, who was snapped up by Oxford United. He was one I remember as a young supporter, but unfortunately for him he never really reached his full potential, in my opinion. Although he was a full Welsh international left back he could have gone to one of the more fashionable clubs back then. It was a shame that he had to finish his career early due to a serious injury.

I did, however, choose Michael Smith, who was brought into

Bristol Rovers by the infamous Paul Buckle, who didn't wash well in his very short spell as manager. But if he deserves any credit, and I don't think there was much that the supporters would thank him for, then he can have some for his purchase of Smith from Ballymena United Northern Ireland in the summer of 2011.

Michael Smith always looked a class above the majority of his teammates during his time at Rovers. He was quick, read the game well and enjoyed getting forward when he could. He was also gifted with a bit of pace, which is always handy. I was sad to see him leave in the summer of 2014 to join Peterborough United in Division One. It would have been nice of him to stay and put right the wrongs of some of his teammates after our relegation into the Conference. It was understandable that he left when he did, as he had his heart set on chasing a Northern Ireland cap. I'm sure he will always be an ex-player who will receive a good hand if he should ever return to play against the famous blue and white quarters in the future.

Next in my line-up is Vaughan Jones. Vaughan Jones had a couple of playing spells at Rovers, playing almost 400 games for the club. His most successful spell would have been lifting the old Third Division title in the 1989/90 season. He also had the thrill of leading Rovers out at the old Wembley Stadium. Jonesie was a reliable defender in his time at the club, and he also had spells with Cardiff City and Newport County before finishing his playing days with Bath City. He was another Welshman at Rovers, who also had an International U21 cap to his name.

That's my back four and goalkeeper sorted out. They're pretty reliable, with strength down the middle, and pace out wide from Smithy. Remember, I would have all these players at their peak.

The midfield: another hard decision to make here. I've actually gone for two midfield generals. Both players could put their foot on the ball, knock a decent pass around the park, and always seem to have that extra bit of time on the ball. I have also gone for two wingers, who I would hope could swap it around from left to right and keep the opposition on their toes.

OK, so first up in the middle is David Williams. This guy was a quality player during his time at Rovers before leaving in a surprise

123

move to Norwich City. David Williams also became the player-manager at the Gas, and he led Rovers to strong finishes in the old Division Three just before the introduction of the play-offs. We just couldn't get over the line back then, but I'm sure a play-off system would have seen us gain that elusive promotion back to the second tier under him.

Alongside David Williams I would install the fighter and neat little dynamo Ian Holloway. What a character he was, and still is. Ian Holloway would get stuck in when he had to, and could play some creative football with the ball at his feet. He was a good guy who motivated the team with his never say die attitude, barking out instructions from the middle. He always could come up with a goal or two in times of need, and he was also known to knock in the vital penalty or two when called upon. Who can ever forget the vital penalty at Prenton Park against Tranmere Rovers in our 1989/90 Championship winning season?

His playing career took him to Queens Park Rangers and the Premiership before his managerial career roundabout started. I was sad to see him leave as a player and manager during his spells with Rovers. I still wouldn't rule out seeing him back at Rovers in some capacity one day. Who knows? So Ian Holloway needs no further introduction as he takes his place in the middle.

My two wingers are from completely different backgrounds. Firstly we have a player who was a local lad, who was just coming into his best form and was just beginning to flourish. The other player I've chosen would have been at the end of his career after playing at the very top level for some of the biggest club sides in both England and Scotland.

My first choice has gone to Mickey Barrett. I was lucky to have had the pleasure of watching him in action during the early 1980s. I remember Mickey Barrett running at players and causing defenders all kinds of trouble as he set out to attack them. It was a massive shock when during the preseason in 1984 Mickey suddenly fell ill and passed away with an aggressive form of cancer. He had probably just begun to play some of his best football in a Rovers shirt and I, for one, was a fan of his intricate wing skills. He starred in the amazing comeback against Millwall at Eastville Stadium when we came from behind to score a late winner, which ultimately set us up with an outside chance of promotion on the last day of the season at Hull City in May 1984. Unfortunately the results didn't go our way on that final Saturday, and we missed out come the end.

The goal Mickey Barrett scored, one that has stuck in my mind for many a year, was a goal he scored at Eastville in a convincing win over Scunthorpe United. I remember him cutting back across the goal from left to right and firing a shot past the keeper up at the Muller Road end of the stadium. I watched it go in from the old Tote End which, if you didn't know, was what seemed like a mile away from the other end of the ground due to the old Bristol Bulldogs speedway track running around the perimeter. So Mickey Barrett takes a place in my side.

The last player who completes my midfield four is Mark Walters. Mark Walters came to Bristol Rovers back in 1992 and was signed by our then manager, Ian Holloway. Mark Walters had been a full England international and had played for some top clubs, namely Aston Villa, Rangers, and Liverpool. He made quite an impact during his time with Bristol Rovers, even though he was at the end of a glittering career. He was also a firm favourite of the fans, as the fans often sang his name.

Wally! Wally Walters! …. Wally! Wally Walters! You could see the class that he had, and he would be able to pass a ball to feet almost without any effort. His dead ball free-kicks were wonderful to watch as he scored a few screamers to the delight of the Memorial Stadium faithful. To have had such a player playing for the blue and white quarters was a joy in my opinion, and it reminded me of the big coup signings that Bobby Gould had carried out back in the 1980s when he signed Mick Channon and Alan Ball.

Choosing my top XI was a difficult task, as I have mentioned earlier, and to come up with a pair of forwards was almost impossible. We have had a string of great strikers over the years that I have been watching Bristol Rovers, and I could have named numerous combinations of players who all would have been worthy of a starting spot. In the end I went for a couple of players who were players in our time at the Memorial Stadium. You may well disagree or agree on

125

these, but I think I could easily change them from one day to the next as it really was that hard to decide.

Making up my front two are Rickie Lambert and Jason Roberts. Rickie Lambert came to Bristol Rovers from Rochdale in 2006 for £200,000. He was a regular in the team, but he had a fairly quiet start to his time at Rovers. He still managed to score some vital goals during this period. Who could forget the screamer against Swindon Town at the Memorial Stadium as we rocketed up the table to snatch our play-off place and ultimate promotion at Wembley in 2007?

Another massive strike was the goal that almost burst the net as he scored against our arch-rivals in the League Trophy Southern Area final, also at the Memorial Stadium, which took us to the final in Cardiff at the Millennium Stadium. And finally I need to mention the late strike away at Hartlepool, when we needed all three points to snatch our play-off spot away from Stockport County.

Jason Roberts was my final choice, and he will partner Rickie Lambert up front. What a combination that sounds. Jason Roberts came to Bristol Rovers in the summer of 1998 after Rovers paid Wolverhampton Wanderers £250,000. Jason Roberts's career really began to take shape after he joined Rovers and partnered Jamie Cureton after Barry Hayles left for Fulham in a £2 million move in November 1998.

Rovers had an abundance of strikers around this period, which also included Nathan Ellington and Bobby Zamora – who all played their own part in what was a very strong side that ultimately never really reached its full potential. If they could have achieved the promotion they deserved then who knows where it could have led for us, as every one of these players went on to spend a period playing Premiership football. You could see that Roberts had an eye for goal. He was a tall, strong and lean skilful player, happy with the ball at feet, or delivered to him to run on to, or met in the box with his head. He had a bit of everything, and you knew he was heading for a higher level of football. It was just unfortunate that it wasn't going to be with us.

That completes my one to eleven, but I thought I might do worse than add a few substitutes to the list, as it was a difficult to overlook these other guys. I could have also added our current striker Matty Taylor to the list. His goalscoring record can't be questioned over the last couple of seasons, and he is definitely one to watch. I would have liked to have added a couple more but I could go on and on, so decided to limit it to just five names. My substitute bench would consist of the following:

Paul Randall – a boyhood hero of mine and a great goal poacher. He scored some vital goals in his time at Rovers and will always be in my list of favourite players ever to wear the famous blue and white quarters,

Vitālijs Astafjevs – a Latvian international during his time at Rovers, and he oozed class. He always found time on the ball, and controlled the middle of the park.

Stuart Campbell – a gritty player who wasn't one to shy away from his responsibilities. He became a firm favourite at Rovers, and it was a shame he left after our relegation from Division One to take up a playing and coaching post at Tampa Bay Rowdies.

Brian Parkin – we all need another goalkeeper on the bench. So I'm going for the reliable Brian Parkin, who took over from where Nigel Martyn left off and was a big piece of the jigsaw that saw us gain promotion to the old Second Division in 1990 and help retain that status for a while thereafter.

David Pritchard – another hard, determined defender, who sadly had to call a day on his career prematurely due to injury.

And as a footnote to these guys above, I would like to compliment and thank the following for their contribution over the years I have followed the Rovers:

Archie Stephens – 1981–85: forty goals in 127 games.

Nathan Ellington – 1999–2002: thirty-five goals in 116 games.

Jamie Cureton – 1996–2000: seventy-two goals in 174 games.

So who is going to take charge of my all-time select XI? The manager has to be none other than Gerry Francis, who led Bristol Rovers through one of the best periods in the club's recent history on a shoestring budget playing outside Bristol. He had very little to work with, but still managed to put together a side who worked their socks off for one another and took Rovers to the Division Three title, along with their first-ever visit to the twin towers of Wembley.

Alongside Gerry Francis I'm going to go for a choice that will be no surprise at all. I'm giving that place to Darrell Clarke. Darrell has only just come on to the scene and he is surely destined for great things. He's now proving his worth as a Football League manager, and what he did during the 2014/15 Conference season and again just twelve months later with another Bristol Rovers promotion from League Two to League One shouldn't be underestimated. Back to back promotions! That takes some doing.

The guy along with the players he assembled had to play under unimaginable pressure from the Bristol Rovers supporters, where a conceded goal was greeted as if your nan had just been fiddled out of her life saving by some con man. He stood up and went about it in a way I'm not sure many others could and showed his true colours and utter relief after that final whistle blew in the Wembley play-off triumph against Grimsby Town. Thank you, Darrell. You brought back a lot of positivity to the football club and engaged well with the supporters.

Who would ever forget watching the two videos doing the rounds on YouTube? The singing at the Vic public house on Gloucester Road and the aftermath, once promotion had been secured, were priceless. However, I hope we never have to go through a season of pressure at that particular level ever again.

My All-Time Bristol Rovers Starting Eleven

Goalkeeper: Nigel Martyn
Defender: Michael Smith
Defender: Gary Mabbutt
Defender: Andy Tillson
Defender: Vaughan Jones

Midfielder: Mark Walters
Midfielder: Ian Holloway
Midfielder: David Williams
Midfielder: Mickey Barrett

Forward: Rickie Lambert
Forward: Jason Roberts

Subs bench:

Paul Randall (forward)
Vitālijs Astafjevs (midfield)
Stuart Campbell (midfield)
Brian Parkin (goalkeeper)
David Pritchard (defender)

Manager: Gerry Francis
Assistant: Darrell Clarke